couriers of grace

My Daughter, the Sacraments, and a Surprising Walk of Faith

"For those of us who have ever taken the sacraments for granted without truly discovering the remarkable grace of sacramental joys all around us, Sarah and Nancy Jo Sullivan serve as our guides to seeing God's bountiful grace all around us. Don a tiara or grab your crown, linger over these lovely pages, and prepare to have your heart expanded and your soul sweetly serenaded."

Lisa M. Hendey
Founder of *CatholicMom.com* and author of
The Handbook for Catholic Moms

"We are constantly surrounded by signs of God's presence, yet so often they go unnoticed. By opening her heart and sharing the intimate story of her daughter Sarah's earthly journey, Nancy Jo Sullivan awakens the reader to the signs and wonders of God in everyday life and, at the same time, draws us into the seven sacraments in a new and profound way. Like the sacraments themselves, *Couriers of Grace* invites us to slow down, encounter Christ and 'breathe in the fragrance of God's unconditional love.' If you've ever wondered where God was during the trivial times, the trials, and the triumphs of your life, this book is a must read!"

Kelly M. Wahlquist
Founder of WINE: Women In the New Evangelization
and editor of *Walk in Her Sandals*

"Anyone who knows and loves a person with special needs will relate to the stories and reflections shared so skillfully by Nancy Jo Sullivan in this book."

David and Mercedes Rizzo
Authors of *Spiritually Able: A Parent's Guide to Teaching
the Faith to Children with Special Needs*

couriers of grace

My Daughter, the Sacraments, and a Surprising Walk of Faith

Nancy Jo Sullivan

AVE MARIA PRESS AVE Notre Dame, Indiana

© 2017 by Nancy Jo Sullivan

Founded in 1865, Ave Maria Press is a ministry of the United States Province of Holy Cross.

www.avemariapress.com

Paperback: ISBN-13 978-1-59471-679-9

E-book: ISBN-13 978-1-59471-680-5

Cover image © .

Cover design by Katherine Robinson.

Text design by Christopher D. Tobin.

Printed and bound in the United States of America.

Library of Congress Cataloging-in-Publication Data is available.

Contents

Introduction

Once Upon a Sacrament

Once upon a time . . .

For most of us, the expression calls to mind the beloved fairy tales of our childhood: Cinderella, Snow White, and Beauty and the Beast. When we hear these words, we know that a beautiful story has begun and our hearts are opened, at least momentarily, to the wonder of true and everlasting love.

Once upon a time . . .

For me, the words trigger memories of someone who transformed my life: my late daughter. Almost thirty years ago, she was born on a snowy Minnesota evening. We named her Sarah, meaning God's princess. Though many years have passed, I remember her arrival like it was yesterday.

At twenty-six years old, I was recovering from labor at St. Joseph's Hospital. As I lay in a hospital bed, I cradled our firstborn. My young husband stood by, wearing a baseball cap and a wide grin.

Like all new parents, we were elated. Young and naive, we didn't see the signs of a disability. "She's so beautiful," we cooed as we counted her fingers and toes. But then a team of doctors began gathering around my bed. They carried clipboards and wrote notes. "I'm sorry," one doctor said. He shook his head as if he was trying to formulate his thoughts. "We've noticed some symptoms, some tendencies . . ." he trailed off, taking off his glasses. As the room grew quiet and still, he looked us in the eye. "We believe your baby has Down syndrome."

I closed my eyes.

Lord, there must be some mistake.

Up until that moment, my faith had been a formula, a prescription of sacred rules I followed without wavering. Having grown up in a large Catholic family, I had come to believe that if I attended Mass every week and received the sacraments regularly, I would somehow escape the heartaches of life. As a child, I attended catechism classes at Nativity of Mary, our home parish. The nuns, dressed in full habit, had taught us the importance of fasting. Every Lent, along with my eight brothers and sisters, we ate tuna casserole on Friday evenings. For six weeks, we gave up chocolate, pop, and *The Brady Bunch*. To me, these sacrifices were like a deposit that could be drawn upon if we needed something special from God. Faith was a predictable rhythm of holy days and seasons.

My mother and father had a cedar chest in their bedroom. The wooden heirloom was filled with photos and artwork along with certificates from our Baptisms, First Communions, and Confirmations. Those documents were important to our family history: a spiritual treasury of obligations fulfilled.

The prayers of my childhood were etched in my memory: the Our Father, Hail Mary, and Glory Be. During my pregnancy I had prayed these prayers each day, making the Sign of the Cross over my womb like an invisible fence of protection. *Lord, let your favor rest upon this child.*

At twenty-six years of age, I had never had any reason to question God. I knew the rules and followed them. But now, as I held our first baby, a quiet terror rose up inside of me. My child's disability could not be prayed away. There wasn't a prayer or sacrament to heal Down syndrome. Sacrifices would never alter my child's mental and physical limitations. For the first time in my life, I heard myself ask, "Why God?"

As I wrestled with this question, something unforgettable happened: the light in the room became extraordinarily bright. It was a transfiguration, of sorts, just like in the scriptures. God was present; it was if he was standing right next to my bed. In the brightness, I heard the Lord say, "This child is a gift."

A few days later, we took our baby home. At that time, we didn't know that Sarah was, indeed, a princess. But how could we have possibly known? God, in his mysterious wonder, had disguised her royal spirit in low muscle tone and slanted eyes that sparkled.

Our enlightenment began almost immediately.

As an infant, Sarah smiled *all* the time.

She never went through her terrible twos, or threes, or fours. She was too busy defying her disabilities as she slowly learned to walk, talk, sing, and dance. As she began learning the alphabet and how to read a few words, she was drawn to fairy tales.

As a little girl, she had bookshelves in her room lined with the classic tales of queens, kings, and castles. I think she identified with the mythical maidens who found true love. All these years later, this makes perfect sense to me. Sarah had a heart full of love and was a princess in every sense of the word. She even had her own crown collection.

One rainy afternoon, I was reading her the story of Snow White along with her two younger sisters. At that time she was about six years old, and our family had grown. As the four of us cuddled together on the couch, Sarah sat next to me, wearing pink glasses that glittered and a little tiara on her head.

When we turned to an illustration of a princess dressed in a beautiful gown, Sarah leaned in and pointed to the princess. "Mom, that's-that's me."

She got up and started dancing around the family room. "I'm loved!" she proclaimed in a happy voice.

As she curtsied and twirled, her sisters and I joined in the dance. An ordinary moment on an ordinary day, but the kingdom of God, with all its beautiful simplicity, was in our midst. Sarah had brought it to us.

Over time, I began to see more and more the power and presence of God at work in the ordinariness of my life. Like Sarah, our two younger daughters arrived with graces to share. Through the three of them, I came to a whole new understanding of what the word "sacrament" means: an outward and visible sign of inward and spiritual divine grace.

As Sarah grew into her teenage years, she became more pensive and started penning her thoughts on the back covers of her fairy tale books. Every afternoon, when she would come home from her special education class, she would dress up in one of the gowns I had picked up for her at Goodwill. Then, with a crown on her head, she would sit at her desk and write misspelled quotes about her life, things like "My nme is Princess Sarah. God lives in my hart. Someday my Prince will come." One day, as I was rushing past her room with a laundry basket, I stopped to take a peek at her work. She had written "I have a pirfect life."

During her twenty-three years on earth, Sarah never once lamented what she couldn't do. Instead, she read love stories. She wrote beautiful messages. She dressed up on ordinary afternoons. She danced. She smiled. She recognized and celebrated the "pirfect" life that God had given her.

Were there times when her disability was hard on me? Did I have moments when I wished everything was different? Of course. But now that Sarah is safe in God's arms, I can't seem to recall the hard days. Maybe that's because I know so much more now than I did as a young mother. Sarah's life, in essence, was a sacrament, a visible sign of God's grace. Through her, God transfigured me, my family, and all those who knew her.

Though my faith was once rooted in a series of certificates and sacrifices, Sarah introduced me to the God who companions with his people, Emmanuel, God with us. The tender God who knows each of our hearts—every hidden fear and failing—and loves us anyway. The God who says, "you are precious in my sight, and honored, and I love you" (Is 43:4).

Part of Sarah's mission, I believe, was to draw me into the seven sacraments and to help me uncover our loving God in tangible things such as light, oil, and sparkling water. My personal shepherdess, she guided me to pastures of insight, leading me to the quiet mercies of the confessional and the still waters of forgiveness. She taught me to cherish wedding dresses and chasubles and to rest in God's promises. She invited me to taste bread and wine as slowly as she did and to see goodness and mercy in this gift.

Sarah recognized her Lord in the seven sacraments but knew that his glory could not be confined to a sacred rite or liturgy. As I watched her grow, and learned from her, I came to understand that life, all of it, is sacrament. In brokenness that turns to blessing, in laughter that eases our pain, and in the silence of hope, God's touch is felt. In all these things, we are sanctified.

It is my hope that this book will speak to all seekers of grace; parents and priests, sinners and saints, old and young, divorced, single, or widowed. Your story, whatever it might be, is inscribed with grace. This is your once upon a time, your moment to discover the dazzle of God.

As you turn these pages, perhaps you will see yourself in these words, in the struggle, joy, and transformation. And perhaps, in the reading, a transfiguration will come.

Chapter 1

Baptism

Diving into the Waters of Life

The truth, even though I cannot feel it right now,
is that I am the chosen child of God, precious in
God's eyes, called the beloved from all eternity,
and held safe in an everlasting belief.
—Henri J. M. Nouwen, *Life of the Beloved*

It's mid-April in Minneapolis. Spring has arrived, and
the sun feels warm on my back. I'm sitting on the
shoreline of Lake Harriet, a scenic beach just a mile
from my home. Surrounded by rose gardens and turn-
of-the-nineteenth-century houses, the lake feels a little
bit like paradise. Lined with towering oaks, memories of
the past linger in these waters. On warm summer mornings when I was a little girl, my mother would pack all
of us kids into our station wagon and drive to the lake.
We splashed in the water, built sand castles, and listened

to the top ten hits playing from a transistor radio. The
sailboats anchored by the shore, clinked in a bay.

For hours we'd swim, all nine of us, jumping off
the dock and searching for colorful rocks under the
water. "I found agates!" my brother Timmy would call
out as he rose from the lake, his hands brimming with
stones that were swirled with pink and yellow quartz
lines. Under this sea, there was a world of wonder: min-
nows, shells, and pebbly sand that massaged our feet.
I, too, would dive under, holding my breath. Paddling
downward, there was only a short window of time to
retrieve the glistening agates that lay on the bottom.
When I could no longer breathe, I shot up for air like a
rocket, my treasures in tow.

After swimming, my mother would unpack nine
peanut butter sandwiches from a cooler, all wrapped in
baggies. She would spread them out on the picnic table,
one for each. With a scarf tied around her hair, Mom
poured Kool-Aid into Dixie cups before the summer
breeze tried to whisk them away. The fragrance of roses
and pine trees filled the air. The sound of the waves lapping against the shore was a hymn that echoed through
the church of summer.

The lake was a sign of God's presence in our lives,
a glimpse of heaven's glory, even though we wouldn't
have called it that then. The sand and sea were ours to
embrace. Like the psalmist once wrote, the voice of the
Lord was "over the waters" (Ps 29:3). At the lake, the
sacredness of life was everywhere. And we were part
of it.

When September came, I grieved the loss of swimming and rock hunting. Right about the time school started, Lake Harriet began dying a slow but breathtakingly beautiful death. The leaves, once lush and green, crumpled like parchment, and the cold winds commanded the lake waters to turn to ice. Then the season of hockey and hot chocolate began.

After the first snowfall, my father began construction of an ice skating rink in our backyard. Under his watchful eye, he made my siblings and I shovel snow from the center of our yard toward the pine trees that hedged our property line. Wearing mittens and puffy jackets, we took turns holding a running hose, the water crystalizing on its way to the frigid ground. A prism of colored water would often flicker from the hose. "It's a rainbow," I called out one day, my breath freezing into a white mist.

We skated through the winter on that bumpy, makeshift rink. Sometimes we played hockey in near-blinding snowstorms. Other times we etched figure eights with our skates. Under the moonlight, we skittered as fast as we could across the ice and pummeled free-falling into the snowbanks. The frozen ice was our playground and saved us from months of indoor imprisonment.

But the waters, too, held dangers. I remember hearing about the kids who drowned in the lakes of Minnesota when I was young—*Had they not had swimming lessons? What had gone wrong?* I wondered.

One winter day when I was ten, the air was getting warmer, and the ice rink in our backyard was beginning to melt. That Saturday afternoon, my siblings were hanging out in the rec room in our basement, watching monster movies. "It's too warm to skate," they told me.

Not wanting to surrender the last days of winter, I laced up my skates and clicked across the street to a pond I thought was frozen. When I stepped onto the ice, I heard a sickening crack.

Oh no . . . I called out for help, but no one heard me. The ice gave way before I could get to the edge, and I sank through. The pond swallowed me up and covered me with icy water.

I knew I had just a short window of time to retrieve my breath. I tried paddling upward, but the blades of my skates weighed me down and the unbroken ice encased me above, darkening the view and leaving only one way out. *If I die, no one will find me*, I panicked.

There were no treasures under these waters. No warmth. No light. Thrashing about, I gasped for absent air. *Please help me, God!*

As I called out to heaven, I sensed that someone or something was hoisting me up, pushing me to a safe edge where I could ease myself out without the ice breaking some more. When my whole body was up on the flat ice, I worked to catch my breath and slither to stronger ice until finally I was standing at the edge of the pond, looking over at the hole I had broken in the ice.

"I've been saved," I whispered, my hair frozen into icy strands.

For years, I never spoke about my brush with death to anyone. I just couldn't find the right words to explain what had happened to me that day. I had encountered God in the water; I knew this. But why had I been saved?

Sixteen years later, on the day of Sarah's Baptism, the answer came.

On that snowy December morning, my young husband, Don, and I stood at the baptismal font in a small chapel. Surrounded by family and godparents, Sarah slept in my arms. It was Advent, and the little church was decorated with tall pine trees and banners of purple.

Sarah was just a few weeks old. She wore a dress of white satin—a christening gown that had been in our family for generations. *She looks like a tiny queen*, I thought. In the light of the stained glass windows, the waters in the font sparkled.

"What name do you give this child?" the priest asked.

"Sarah Marie," Don and I proclaimed.

Sarah's regal gown could not veil her disability. Sleeping soundly, her slanted eyes were closed, and her flaccid arms flopped to her side like a little rag doll. Before my labor pains began, before Sarah took her first breath, before the doctors began explaining that our firstborn had an extra chromosome, and before so many dreams had been shattered, we had carefully chosen our daughter's name: Sarah, which means "God's princess."

"What do you ask of God's Church?"

"Baptism" we replied.

It was the right answer, of course. The answer that all Catholic parents give when they bring their children to the font. But the answer I gave to the priest seemed incomplete at best. Don and I were first-time parents,

young and naive. We didn't know how to raise any
child, let alone a "special" child. We needed so much
more from our Church than a Baptism. We needed our
Church to wrap their arms around us and say, "We are
here for you. Everything will be OK."

The priest went on with the Rite: "It will be your
duty to bring her up to keep God's commandments as
Christ taught us, by loving God and our neighbor. Do
you clearly understand what you are undertaking?"

"We do."

As I brushed Sarah's face, I wanted to recant what I
had just said. *No Lord, we don't clearly understand what we
are undertaking! How will we teach her the Ten Commandments if you haven't given her the ability to understand them?*

I turned my glance toward my two sisters who had
recently given birth. They stood next to me at the baptismal font cradling their non-disabled babies. I wanted to
feel their joy. I wanted to know what it might be like to
take a newborn home from the hospital and not worry
about things such as special schools, open heart surger-
ies, or physical therapy sessions. All I wanted to be that
day was an un-special mother.

I watched as the priest dipped his hand into the
font and said, "We ask you, Father, with your Son to
send the Holy Spirit upon the water of this font. May all
who are buried with Christ in the death of baptism rise
also with him to newness of life. We ask this through
Christ our Lord."

As water was poured over Sarah's forehead, her
eyes opened as she awoke, wiggling and squirming
in my arms. As my eyes met hers, I saw myself being

immersed in the font. Sinking into the water, I tried to paddle upward but the heaviness of grief weighed me down. *Oh no!*

In my mind's eye, I thrashed about. I gasped for air that wasn't there. But who could hear my cries for help?

I closed my eyes and thought of the mother I would have to be. *This will be so much harder than my sisters' roads. I will have to give up so much more of life, and I don't want to. Why did you do this, Lord? Why to her? Why to me and Don? I don't want to die to myself, not this much! Why couldn't she be the healthy little princess we imagined? Why didn't you save her and me from this?*

As the water trickled in the font, I tried my best to give the Lord my dreams in exchange for God's holy and perfect plan.

This is so hard.

And in those moments, it felt like something was hoisting me up.

You weren't meant to stay in the water, an inner voice prompted.

Afterward, I couldn't find the right words to explain what had happened to me in that moment. All I knew was that I had encountered the Lord.

Don drew near, holding Sarah's baptismal candle. In the warmth of candlelight, Sarah's face sparkled, and the priest said, "This child of yours has been enlightened by Christ. She is to walk always as a child of the light. May she keep the flame of faith alive in her heart. When the Lord comes, may she go out to meet him with all the saints in the heavenly kingdom."

I held Sarah close. With misting eyes, I suddenly realized why God had rescued me as child. I had been saved for this miraculous moment. By all appearances, Sarah was the "least" in God's kingdom, but the waters of Baptism marked her as royalty. She was the child of a king, God's princess, and in that moment, I realized I needed to learn from her.

I watched as the priest traced the Sign of the Cross on Sarah's forehead. "The God of power and Father of our Lord Jesus Christ has freed you from sin, given you a new birth by water and the Holy Spirit." Sarah's Baptism was a coronation. Crowned with life-giving water and anointed to serve, her regal mission had begun. She had been empowered to lead me, Don, and everyone she encountered on earth into the kingdom of God.

In that moment, I imagined myself wearing a laurel, too. This was Sarah's baptismal day, yes, but I felt a sprinkling of grace, too. God was pulling me from the font of fear. He was reviving me, planting my feet on the hallowed ground of hope. I had no idea what lay ahead, but I could move forward now, step by step and prayer by prayer. I had been saved to protect and nurture this anointed one. Like Sarah, and all other baptized believers, I wasn't meant to stay in the water. On this day of light, my new mission had just begun.

Now that I'm a much older mother, sitting on the shoreline of Lake Harriet, I'm listening to the sound of the waves lapping against the shore. The rhythm of the water hasn't changed since I was young; it still sounds so calming.

This lake always makes me a little nostalgic. As I watch the sailboats, I'm remembering a summer day that I spent with Sarah at this beach—she was around ten years old then—along with her two younger sisters, Christina and Rachael.

On this same shore, I watched as Sarah danced in the lake, paddling about in the shallows with her hands in the sand, her legs free and flowing. Meanwhile little Christina and Rachael dove for agates near the dock. "Mom, we found some pink rocks" my youngest called out to me.

"I can't wait to see what you've found!" I called back, a warm breeze blowing through my hair.

By that time, I had gotten used to the sacrifices that all parents, and especially parents of special children, must offer. There had been endless meetings with Sarah's teachers. Don and I were in constant contact with therapists and doctors. People often stared at Sarah when we went out in public as a family. Little Christina and Rachael were learning, at a very early age, that some people can be cruel and insensitive to the disabled. They, too, had been baptized in Christ; they accepted their older sister just as she was, and they were growing in their own delightful, compassionate natures and faith.

Motherhood hadn't gone according to my plan, that's for sure. But I was learning to accept the mystery of Sarah's life and discovering, to my surprise, that it was possible to rest in the questions of life.

Like all of my children, Sarah was a sign of God's presence in our family, a glimpse of heaven's glory. Though I loved each of my children equally, Sarah's life had a special quality and beauty that sprang, in part, from her limitations. She seemed undistracted from the typical worries of the world and knew, on a deep and profound level, that she bore the brightness of Christ. The joy that beamed from her smile was the sunlight of our home.

"Mom, I-I can sing like Ariel." Sarah called out, her stuttered words echoing. Back then, Sarah was a devoted fan of the Disney's *The Little Mermaid* and was quite fond of the sea princess who longed to become fully human. The waves that now surrounded Sarah glittered like diamonds—the only jewels she needed to get into character.

On the shore, I unpacked four peanut butter sandwiches from a cooler, placed them on a picnic table, and began pouring Kool-Aid into Dixie cups. "Go ahead Sarah, I'm listening," I said.

With her head above the water and her hair dripping wet, Sarah began singing "Ah" over and over again, just like Ariel, the inflections in her voice rising to a grand crescendo: "Ah . . . Ah . . . Ah . . . Ah . . . ah . . . Ahhhhhhhhhhh . . ."

This was Sarah's alleluia, a hymn that rang through the chapel of summer. She was fully human, fully alive in Christ. And so were we.

What a beautiful image of Baptism.

Above the waters, in the sunlight of salvation, we encounter the glory of God.

Above the waters, we find our life.

Chapter 2

Reconciliation

The Sweet Sound of Grace

The worst prison would be a closed heart.
—St. John Paul II

As a teenager, I was always at war with my mother. Like two knights suited in armor, we constantly clashed. My grades needed to improve. My eyeliner was too heavy. The music that played from my stereo was always too loud. "Your room looks like a cyclone struck it" she would say.

"So what!" I would retort.

We wielded our words like swords, each of us masters of defense.

I wanted my mother to be like Carol Brady on *The Brady Bunch*, the super-sugary mom who offered nonstop support to her three daughters. I wanted my mother to be my confidante and longed for her

to understand the awkwardness and the uncertainty that defined my adolescent years. I wanted her to
notice the things I was doing well. With nine children,
though, she was too busy to meet these desires. Often
I took care of my younger brothers and sisters, made
dinner on the nights when she couldn't, and tidied up
the house when it was messy.

I wondered what it would be like to receive a hug
from her, even once in a while. But Mom was focused
on the basics of family life: making sure we were fed,
clothed, and taken to our many activities.

I had a better relationship with my dad. Beginning when I was a little girl and lasting well into my
teenage years, Dad and I had a regular morning routine. Every morning, long before the rest of the family
was up, I would join him at the kitchen table. There,
he would tell me stories of a mythical princess named
Ko-Jo. Coincidently, Ko-Jo had the same nickname as
I did!

While coffee percolated in an olive green pot, I
leaned in and listened to Dad's version of my namesake:
"Ko-Jo wore a buckskin skirt with fringe, and her crown
was a laurel of leaves . . ."

During those early mornings, I saw myself in
those stories and believed, for just a moment, that I
was royalty. Sometimes Dad would take quick gulps
of coffee and begin tapping his hands on the table,
imitating the sound of a drum: "Close your eyes,
Nance. Can you see Ko-Jo dancing underneath the
stars?"

"Yes. Yes, Dad, I can," I would call out, twirling in my mind's eye.

But everything changed in the evening when Dad came home from work. After eating dinner with the family, he would leave the kitchen table and quietly make his way to the den off our upstairs hallway. For the rest of the night, he would sit alone in the darkness of that den drinking a twelve pack of Special Export beer. I often wondered why he drank. *Was he still sad that his own father had passed away when he was only a teen?* As I walked passed his closed door each night, I never reached a conclusion.

After high school, I went away to St. Catherine's, an all-girls Catholic college in Saint Paul, Minnesota. Secretly, I was glad to leave all the confusion that filled my home. Dad continued drinking while I began studying the effects of alcoholism in a psychology class. At the advice of a trusted professor, I contacted a local treatment center and began realizing that Dad needed more help than our family could give him.

One day, I called my mother from my dorm room and started to explain what I had learned. "Dad can't stop drinking on his own. Let's schedule a family meeting, Mom."

Initially my mother agreed to an intervention and, surprisingly, so did my father. But neither of them showed up to the meeting, and only a few of my brothers and sisters were there. Later my mother called me and said, "Your father will be fine. Don't mess things up."

Dad passed away a few years later, before he could ever try a new way of life or experience a new future. He never had time to get to know Sarah, Christina, or Rachael. After Dad died, Mom's attention turned even further from me and my siblings. Now, she focused on grieving Dad's death and repackaging her future. Meanwhile, I tried to sort through all that had and hadn't happened during my growing up years, all the while muddling my way through marriage problems and raising young children. Though I told myself I was fine, I still felt such anger, and my hurt remained unresolved. Dad was gone, and in many ways, so was Mom.

* * *

When Sarah was about seven years old, she called her younger sister a blockhead. Don and I were shocked; she had never uttered an unkind word before that point. The incident happened immediately after she and her sisters had watched a Charlie Brown special on television, one in which Charlie Brown received the familiar insult again and again.

"Sarah, you never call someone a name," I told her as I looked her straight in the eye. She crossed her arms in sweet defiance. "Ask Christina for forgiveness," I instructed.

With her pink glasses sliding down her nose, she turned to Christina and stuttered, "S-s-s-s-sorry, blockhead." Don and I turned away, trying to muffle our laughter.

Sarah rarely sinned, at least not in a grave way. But as she watched the interactions of Charlie Brown's friends and viewed her fairy tales on videos, she would imitate the characters she had come to know so well.

One afternoon, I noticed little Sarah lying on her bed like Cleopatra lounging on a chaise. Decked out in one of my old prom dresses, eyes tightly closed, and crown nearly falling off her head, she clutched a plastic apple in her right hand and looked as though she, like Snow White, had been poisoned by an evil stepmother.

"Sarah, are you OK?" I asked.

She quickly woke up and giggled: "I'm just-just pretending, Mom. I get to wake up now." With that, she dramatically dropped the apple, and I watched it roll underneath her dresser, out of sight. "Never eat a p-p-poisoned apple!" she told me.

I believe that Sarah's fairy tales helped her to understand the difference between good and evil. Snow White was Sarah's hero, and she often emulated her kindness. If Sarah was given a cookie, she would break it into pieces to share with her sisters. If someone made an unkind remark about her appearance, she would smile and wave at him. Each day she would sing the lyrics to her favorite Disney love songs, performing for us in the living room with a toy microphone. With every stuttered verse, Sarah invited us into the purity of her world, a place where wishes, hopes, and dreams always came true.

After talking with Sarah's doctor about her imitational nature, he explained that mimicry is common in Down syndrome children. "Sarah may observe others and reproduce their gestures, speech, and actions," he told us.

Another trait we noticed in Sarah was her stubbornness. This became more apparent when we began to limit her sugar intake. Like many Down syndrome kids, she had low muscle tone, and we were always watching her weight.

"Sarah, you can have one treat a day, just one," I used to say.

One night, after midnight, I heard the sound of the kitchen cupboards opening and closing. When I came down the stairs, Sarah was sitting at the kitchen table with five Swiss cake rolls lined up before her. There were cellophane wrappers everywhere.

"Mom, will you f-f-f-forgive me?" she asked. Her mouth was completely stuffed with cake and there were crumbs all over her face. She bowed her head, as if I were a queen who could grant her absolution. "Yes, Sarah," I said firmly, "but you can't keep sneaking treats." I heard myself begin to laugh as she looked longingly at her chocolate treasures. I tried desperately to hide my chuckles. "Tastes g-g-good," she said as she happily handed me one of the cakes. It was the best midnight snack I ever had.

When she was old enough to receive the sacrament of Reconciliation, Don and I felt hesitant to register her for classes at our parish. We wondered if Sarah's dramatic tendencies could be considered sins or whether they were merely symptoms of her disability. Could she fully comprehend matters of penance and absolution? She wasn't like most of us. Sarah saw God as a prince who would one-day gallop into her life on a white horse. Her daily thoughts were consumed with castles and kingdoms of love; and unlike other children, she probably wouldn't grow out of this. Stealing, lying, cheating, swearing, and placing the world's pleasures before God were not parts of her daily life.

Was it her disability or her innate goodness that made her so Christlike? We could never be sure. How were we to introduce the concept of sin and judgment to someone who, seemingly without any effort, was so kind and compassionate?

Then there was also her speech impediment. Even if she had the ability to name her transgressions, how could she articulate her sins to a priest?

"God knows Sarah's heart," Don said one evening as we ate dinner at the kitchen table. I nodded in agreement. "I don't think she's capable of hurting anyone," I added. We didn't want to risk the possibility that she might change her beloved God and prince into a judger of sins. Yes, Christina and eventually Rachael would need help to understand the more complex principles of absolution, but Sarah was best with her childlike faith. After much discussion, we decided not to have her receive the sacrament.

Still, I felt guilty, especially when Christina and then Rachael came of age and began studying the sacrament of Reconciliation at their Catholic school. On the night before Christina's first Confession, she sat at the kitchen table reviewing a sheet titled "Examination of Conscience for Children." Wearing pajamas and furry slippers, Christina rested her chin on her hand as she stared at the sheet.

"Mom, look at all these sins," she moaned with a loud sigh. Sarah and Rachael sat on either side of their sister, both of them dressed in pink bathrobes.

The questions on the sheet were designed to help children review their failings. But as I read through the list, I took a mental inventory of my own transgressions:

- Have I fooled around at Mass?
- Do I hurt people by calling them names?
- Did I do what my mom and dad told me to do? My teacher? My grandparents?
- Did I do my chores?
- Have I started fights with my brothers and sisters at home?
- Did I lie, cheat, or take something that didn't belong to me?
- Have I forgiven people? Or am I holding a grudge?

As Christina began jotting down her sins, I heard an inner voice say, "You haven't forgiven your parents." I quickly dismissed the prompting and turned my motherly attention to Christina. Wrapping my arms around her, I said, "Honey, God loves you, no matter what. That's what Confession is all about."

Sarah was listening intently to our conversation and added, "F-f-f-forgive!"

She spoke the word with confidence, in a voice so loud that we all stopped what we were doing. "F-f-for-give," she repeated, looking each of us in the eye, one by one. Though Sarah had never received formal instruction in matters of Reconciliation, perhaps God had enlightened her in other ways. Sarah wanted us to know that forgiveness held more power than a long list of sins.

The next evening, the second-grade children, along with their families, gathered together in the church to receive the sacrament. As candles on the altar were lit and the lights in the church were dimmed, a guitarist played soft music near the altar. Dressed in her school uniform, Christina held her head high as she made her way to a confessional just steps away from our pew.

"You'll do just fine," I assured her.

Sarah sat right next to me, coloring a picture of Jesus. Don and Rachael were at a hockey game, and I was grateful for the stillness. In the quiet, the musician began strumming "Amazing Grace" on his guitar. I whispered the lyrics of the ancient hymn: "Amazing Grace how sweet the sound, that saved a wretch like me . . ." I felt my eyes begin to close, and in my mind's eye, I saw my mother's face.

After all these years, was I still harboring bitterness toward her? Was I still angry at Dad for drinking and dying before he could turn his life around or know my children? Did I need to forgive myself for not being able to forgive my parents?

Tears quietly fell from my eyes. *If I go to Confession, I won't be able to speak*, I thought. I hadn't been to

Confession in years, mostly because I didn't want to confront the resentment that stormed within me

Did I even remember the act of contrition that I had learned as a child? "Dear God . . . I'm heartily sorry . . ." Was that how the prayer started? Maybe I could take a peek at the pamphlet with the act of contrition that Christina had just memorized. I think she had left it on the pew.

The confessional was only a few steps away.

"Just go," I told myself.

Sarah laid her head on my shoulder and placed her hand on mine. Comfort flowed from her spirit to mine, and a great calmness came over me.

"'Tis grace that brought me safe thus far, and grace will lead me home."

Christina tiptoed back to our pew. "How did it go?" I whispered.

"I did good, Mom," she said, and I knew she had. And for that moment, that was all I needed.

As we walked out of the church, we passed the confessional door. I would try again on a more courageous day. It would be years until I would return to the sacrament.

* * *

As I busied myself with motherhood, I became a sort of supermom. I made savory dinners and kept up with the nonstop laundry. I chauffeured the kids to their athletic events and sewed matching dresses for my daughters every Christmas and Easter. I was the great caregiver, always one step ahead of Sarah's daily needs.

But I carried my unforgiveness toward my parents like my daughters carried their backpacks. Yes, my mother and I talked regularly. Every Saturday morning, she would call and say, "Let's go to a garage sale," or "How about lunch?" or "There's a craft sale in town." I never considered why I always wanted to cut our time short.

By the time Sarah was a teenager, God had given her the ability to read my deepest thoughts. I often thought that she was a barometer that could measure the pressures in my soul. Sometimes she would draw near after I had spent the morning with my mom. Like a sage, she would turn my face to hers so that she could look at me right in the eye and say, "F-forgive."

I didn't know it then, but I was disabled. Unlike Sarah, my disability was bitterness, and it was a larger impediment than Down syndrome. One rainy afternoon, however, Sarah brought my hidden disability to light.

As it thundered outside our living room window, Christina was angry because her father and I wouldn't let her use the car to go to the mall. She had recently gotten her driver's license and was excited to drive on her own without having a parent tag along. "The weather is too dangerous," I told her firmly.

Sarah and Rachael sat on the couch, watching the unfolding drama as though they were in a theatre. Christina and I battled, wielding our invisible swords. "You don't understand how important this is to me," Christina yelled. "It's too dangerous for you to drive," I shot back. As mother and daughter, we had become masters of defending our own causes. For Rachael and Sarah, it was entertainment to see who would win this latest fencing round.

As the lightning flashed, Christina shouted, "I'm running away!"

She stomped up the wooden stairs, and we could hear her closet doors opening and slamming shut. Minutes later, she stood at the front door clutching a backpack filled with clothes. "I'm leaving," she called out, making the announcement like she was the gruff conductor of a departing train.

"F-f-f-forgive!" Sarah bellowed as the heavy rain pummeled over our roof.

Sarah's admonition came from the depths of her soul, and for a moment, we were silenced.

As we waited to see who would make the next move, Christina whispered something to Sarah before leaving and forcefully slamming the front door. From the living room window, I watched her run down the street, her ponytail blowing in the wind.

I should have run after her. I should have caught up with her and held her protectively in my arms. But in that moment, I was held hostage by memories. Over the years, Don and I had diverted so much of our attention to Sarah's disability—her daily care plans, her ongoing doctor appointments and visits from therapists, and all her special education activities—that we had failed to see how good, how very good, Christina was.

At sixteen years old, she was an honor roll student. Even though Christina was three years younger than

Sarah, she had taken on the role of the oldest sibling, willingly watching over Sarah whenever I needed to run errands. Now that she had her license, she enthusiastically volunteered to drive her younger sister, Rachael, to soccer and hockey practice and helped both of her siblings with homework. She often started dinner and did the wash. She had been doing everything right, and I had been too busy to notice. In storming out of the house, she had been trying to get my attention.

A thunder clap shook the house, and I suddenly realized that I was more like my mother than I wanted to admit. The hard stuff of life had distracted me from Christina and her unique gifts and talents; I began to understand why my mother wasn't there for me when I needed her most. *She was preoccupied*, I thought.

I turned to Sarah. "Where did Christina go?" I asked.

"S-s-s-she went to Starbucks," Sarah replied, proud she was able to offer such classified information.

Minutes later, I was sitting with Christina in the coffee shop. Her sweatshirt was sopping wet, and her hands were shaking. "Mom, the lightning was so scary," she admitted. My teenage daughter still looked like a little girl, her freckled face polished with leftover raindrops and her eyes wide and vulnerable like a child again—my child.

I placed my hand on hers, and I could feel how cold she was. "Will you forgive me for not noticing how beautiful you are?" I asked Christina. "For not telling you how important you are to me and that sometimes I get scared that I will lose you?"

Overcome with emotion, she couldn't speak for a moment. "Yes," she finally whispered, her eyes locked into mine. As the barista brought us cups of hot chocolate, it felt as though God was covering us with a blanket he had preheated for this moment of reconciliation, his loving presence cozy and warm.

"I love you," I told her.

"I love you, too, Mom," she said.

A few months later, I went to Confession.

As I waited in line for the sacrament, I studied the faces of the people waiting with me: an aged man holding a rosary, a fidgeting teenage boy in a letter jacket, a young woman with curly hair reading her Bible. Our stories were different and our reasons for coming to this sacrament were as varied as we were, but we all had something in common: we were seeking the unconditional grace and forgiveness of God.

When I walked into the confessional, a screen afforded anonymous identity, but I chose—I might say courageously—to sit on a chair facing the priest.

"It's taken me a long time to get here," I told the priest. "About twenty years."

"That's OK," he said congenially. "God doesn't mind waiting."

I wasn't reprimanded for my absence from the sacrament, and I was grateful.

As I began sharing my story, I confessed the years I had spent resenting my mom and how I now saw my own failings in a whole new light. As a parent, I'd made many poor choices, too, not the least of which was missing the wonder of Christina and, to some extent, Rachael, too.

I heard myself say, "My mother did the best she could." Yes, she enabled my dad's drinking, but in those days, she simply didn't know what to do. No one really did. Al-Anon groups were just beginning to start in many communities, and the concept of getting help for alcoholism was hard for Mom to understand. So she ran away, and I ran away from her, and years later, Christina ran away from me.

"Is your mother still alive?" the priest asked.

"Yes, but she's getting on in years."

The priest nodded his head as if he understood. "My parents are in their eighties. Sometimes the best we can do is to forgive and enjoy the time we have left with them." It felt as if his family story was similar to mine. "Your penance is to pray five Hail Marys and love your mother as Christ would."

As I began reciting the act of contrition, the words flowed as if I was back in the second grade: "God, I am heartily sorry for having offended thee. . . ."

The storm was over. The bombastic thunder of bitterness had passed, and the lightning of God's mercy had brought new light.

"I absolve you from your sins," I heard the priest pray.

Absolve.

The word means to make free from guilt.

For the first time in many years, I felt free.

* * *

When I remember that; life-changing Confession, I always think of Sarah and cherish her promptings to forgive. Sarah gave us a glimpse of God's incomprehensible mercy and grace. She taught us how to drop the apples that poison our lives: bitterness, unresolved anger, and the refusal to forgive. Through her, we learned to stop clutching our hurts and instead let them roll into the hands of God.

In the holy scriptures, we read, "Therefore be imitators of God . . . and live in love" (Eph 5:1–2). Sarah proclaimed, lived, and shared forgiveness throughout her short life, and in doing so, she imitated the love of our Lord. We, as baptized believers, are called to do the same.

But for most of us, emulating God's love can be challenging, especially when it comes to forgiveness. Jesus says that we are required show mercy not seven times but seventy-seven times (see Matthew 18:21–22). If we are true followers of Christ, we must forgive again and again and again, even if the behaviors of our loved ones remain unchanged.

My relationship with my mother is still less than perfect. Now that she's in her mid-eighties, her health has diminished, and in many ways, she's completely dependent on me and my siblings, which can be very hard. She's still stubborn and often says she's fine even though she needs assistance with most everything: walking, shopping, laundry, eating, and combing her hair. But recently, as my mother and I waited together in the lobby of the doctor's office, I noticed her hands were trembling. "Mom, are you OK?" Given my mother's hearing impairment, I spoke so loudly that my voice reverberated through the lobby like a radio turned to full blast.

"Sometimes I get scared at the doctor," she confessed, hands still trembling. At this point everyone in the lobby was listening to our broadcasted conversation.

"I know, Mom; waiting is hard."

I placed my hand on hers. Then, closing my eyes, I silently prayed, "Lord heal her. Heal me."

Soon my mother stopped shaking, and her entire body began to relax. "What just happened?" my mother asked, her brow furrowed.

"I don't know Mom, maybe the Lord is here."

"Hummph," she grunted, a little untrustingly.

I rolled my eyes. She would never be the best mom, and I, of course, would never be the best daughter. But as I looked into her eyes, now framed by wrinkles and thick-lensed glasses, I heard Sarah whisper, "F-f-forgive!"

In that moment, my mother simply wouldn't let go of my hand.

Much to my delight, I wouldn't let go of hers.

Chapter 3

Eucharist

Broken but Blessed

To one who has faith, no explanation is necessary.
To one without faith, no explanation is possible.
—Thomas Aquinas

Not far from where I live, a grand cathedral over-looks the city of Saint Paul. In the back of the copper-domed church, past the marble statues, chandeliers, and paintings, is a small worship space tucked into an alcove: the Chapel of the Blessed Virgin Mary.

Whenever I need to have an important conversation with God, I find myself kneeling in that sacred hideaway. The space is softly lit, and the design speaks to my love for beauty. In the summertime, the altar is set with a floral cloth and fragrant flowers that delight each prayerful visitor. On curved walls of white are four stained glass windows that catch the sunlight. In mosaic panels of glass, Mary's colorful story is told: a glorious visit from Gabriel, the birth of Jesus, the Crucifixion of her son, and her assumption into heaven.

The sacred images give me pause. Like Mary, all of us have a mixture of brokenness and blessing in our lives.

When I look at the stained glass windows of my life, I like seeing the joyous reflections: my wedding day, the births of my children, and those unforgettable days reserved for sacramental celebrations. Sarah's First Communion is one of my favorite panes. On that spring morning, our family sat in a sunlit pew, all of us decked out for the occasion. Sarah's white veil flowed from the crown of pearls on her head while Christina and Rachael donned matching dresses. Don looked handsome in his suit and tie, and I wore a white pantsuit and pumps.

"Today, we welcome our First Communicants and their families," said the priest.

That morning, the church was packed with families and out of town guests. When it came time for Communion, hundreds of joyful voices joined together to sing the Communion hymn. Honestly, it felt like heaven.

Joining a long line of parents and children, Don and I processed down the center aisle with Sarah. Like all the other parents, we had spent weeks preparing our child to receive the sacrament. As we drew closer to the altar, Sarah began to sway her head back and forth, and I knew what was coming next. Whenever Sarah heard music she danced. It didn't matter if she was listening to a song on the car radio or a CD player or even the lively refrains of a commercial. Music moved her.

The night before, as I tucked her into bed, I told her, "Sarah, tomorrow there will be music at Mass. Try really, *really* hard to stay still." Sarah bowed her head in thought, as if weighing the pros and cons of my request. "M-mom, yes I-I-will t-try."

As on most evenings, Christina and Rachael sat with us on Sarah's bed, all of us dressed in our pajamas. Sarah's room was a regular gathering space for us girls. Underneath a shelf filled with Sarah's crown collection, the four of us would often cuddle on a double bed with an antique headboard. In the light of a princess lamp, we would read fairy tales and stories from the Bible.

That evening, I passed around a cross to the kids. Opening a Bible, I began reading the story of the Last Supper and the Crucifixion of Christ. Listening intently, the girls lounged on the bed.

I wasn't sure how much Sarah comprehended. Christina had already made her First Communion, and Rachael was studying the sacrament at the Catholic school she attended. My non-disabled daughters knew these stories by heart, but I wondered what was going through Sarah's mind.

"Jesus died for you," Christina told Sarah, her words motherly. Rachael dozed off and laid her head on my lap.

In the quietness, I began realizing how little I understood about the sacrament. Like all Catholic kids, I had learned about the Incarnation. God became human. It was such a lofty concept, a Catholic cliché that was repeated in our religion classes but never really understood by those of us who heard it. On the night before God died, he broke bread and became bread.

What did this mean? The nuns who taught us explained that God was present in bread and wine, but how? Was he in these elements physically or just present in a spiritual sense?

I knew the Liturgy of the Eucharist by heart because I'd been repeating it at Mass for years. I could easily recite certain parts of it:

> At the time he was betrayed
> and entered willingly into his Passion,
> he took bread and, giving thanks, broke it,
> and gave it to his disciples, saying:
> take this, all of you, and eat of it,
> for this is my Body,
> which will be given up for you.

The words called to mind images of a wooden cross, iron nails, and the clink of a hammer. I often asked myself why an all-powerful, omnipotent God would allow himself to become broken. Christ had to suffer and die as it was part of a divine plan; I knew this. But surely, I thought, God could have chosen a less violent way to secure forgiveness of sins and eternal life for his people. As a practicing Catholic, I was called to believe a stupendous mystery of faith. God, our suffering Savior, was truly and unequivocally present in bread and wine. How was I to explain this to my children, especially Sarah?

I lifted Sarah's chin, and made sure she was looking into my eyes. "Sarah, tomorrow morning, when you
eat the bread and drink the wine, Jesus will be with
you." It was the best I could do.

Sarah nodded and drifted off to sleep. "I-I- know,
Mom."

These things were in the back of my mind as Sarah
twirled her way toward the altar, her arms flowing to
the music of the Communion hymn. She was like young
John the Baptist, leaping inside Elizabeth's womb. The
pearls on her crown twinkled in the sunlight as brightly
as her smile. Joy welled up in Sarah's spirit like a spar-
kler on the Fourth of July. There was nothing Don or I
could do to contain it.

When it was her turn to receive the Bread of Life,
she dramatically curtsied before the priest.

"Body of Christ," he told Sarah.

For a moment, time seemed to stand still. Sarah
looked at the Host with wide eyes, as if she was seeing
something that everyone else had missed. She chomped
on the Bread slowly, closing her eyes for a few seconds.
As the eucharistic minister handed her the cup, she took
a big swig. After the gulp, she appeared to be in great
thought. Standing near the altar, I clutched Sarah with
one hand and took the Host into my other.

"Body of Christ." the priest said.

"Amen" I replied, and Don followed me.

As we walked back to our pew, I wanted to put on
a pair of sunglasses to hide my identity. Sarah's enthu-
siasm for the Eucharist was on display for the whole
church to see, and I felt embarrassed. Many people in

the pews were smiling at Sarah as if they were seeing something much deeper than her disability, though. Some were even tearing up.

Sarah tugged my arm and asked, "Mom, how-how-how did I do?"

"You did great," I told her.

It was all so awkward and imperfect. Bread chomped. Blood gulped. A child with disabilities dancing toward the altar. Years later, I would recall this moment and my spirit would finally understand just how profound it really was.

* * *

The weeks and months grew into years, as time always does. Our little daughters turned into young teens, and soon our weekly schedule was overloaded with their school activities and sports events. Making time for Mass was like squeezing an SUV into a space reserved for compact cars. There wasn't enough room in our lives for God.

Every Sunday, our family walked down the aisle to receive Communion, but our thoughts were distracted by homework, upcoming doctor appointments, meal preparation, school conferences, play practices, athletic events, and cleaning the house. "Body of Christ," the priest said as the unconditional gift was given, week after week. "Amen" we replied, dutifully.

Sometimes we left church early to attend a hockey game or a tennis match or to drop Sarah off at a special activity. Receiving the sacrament of the Eucharist felt like picking up fast food. We ate and drank the Gift on the run.

During those days, the kids took center stage. As Don and I invested our emotional, spiritual, and physical energy in three children, one with special needs, we ignored the special needs in our marriage. As a couple, there were stories in our past that we didn't have the time or energy to talk about. The truth was, Don and I were disabled in ways that neither us wanted to admit. Like many other husbands and wives, our relationship was unraveling, and we didn't know how to re-seam the threads.

Our divorce was finalized when the girls were teenagers.

After Don moved into his new home, the girls and I found a comforting refuge in Sarah's room as we always had before. Every evening we cuddled together on her bed and talked through the changes that had come to our family. Instead of explaining the complexities of our failed marriage, which they wouldn't have understood anyway, I listened to their fears and offered awkward reassurances. "Will Dad be OK? Will we be OK? Mom . . . will you be OK?" they asked.

With every yes, I closed my eyes and absorbed the very real and palpable pain that divorce brings. "Yes, we are still a family. Yes, Dad will always be in our lives. Yes, our home, our way of life is safe."

I never once told the girls that their father and I were no longer in love. Part of the reason for this was my own conviction that love, at least the love that is outlined in the scriptures, lasts forever. So rather than explaining the details of a lost love, I prayed that God would heal our family.

During those evening discussions, Sarah would page through her fairy tales and study illustrations of happy princes and princesses. I wondered how she and my two other daughters were interpreting the divorce. One evening, Sarah looked up from her book. "T-true love is forever," she said, her eyes magnified beneath her glasses.

Yes, Sarah.

As we adjusted to our new lives, the girls and I continued to attend Mass every Sunday. But we never sat in the main part of the church. Instead, we sat in the back of the church in a space lined with windows and French doors that overlooked the worship area. It was a little alcove set aside for the aged and disabled.

Living in a small town, everyone seemed to know that Don and I had divorced. When we went to Mass, people would often look at us with pity or ask questions we simply didn't want to answer. But in the back of the church, amid the wheelchairs, oxygen tanks, and canes, we felt complete acceptance. During the sign of peace, the elderly parishioners would hug my children and engage them in conversation. When the hymns played through the sound system, Sarah would rock back and forth in her chair and smile. "It-it sounds beautiful," Sarah would loudly whisper.

At Communion time, the eucharistic ministers brought the Body and Blood to us. I was relieved that there was no need to walk down the long aisle toward the altar. In that protected alcove, I could quietly ponder the hurts that had been dormant in my memory since childhood. I prayed for Don, for the kids, for our future. Sometimes, I felt like the Samaritan woman in John's gospel, the divorcee who came to draw water from well at noon, her life in shards. Like me, she kept her stories to herself and her distance from others. Yet as I peered through the glass of the French doors, I saw people of all ages doing exactly what I was doing: praying, reading the scriptures, and singing hymns. Why had they come to Mass? Did they have stories of brokenness, too? Were they thirsting for the Lord, as I was, hoping to find the wellspring of his presence? Sometimes, as I took the Eucharist into my hands, I felt strangely connected with all the people who sat in the church. *We are all on this journey together*, I thought.

One Sunday morning, as the eucharistic ministers made their way to the back of the church, Sarah gripped my hand tightly. "I-I-I want to *go* to Communion, Mom." she said, pointing to the French door.

Christina and Rachael stood up as if they were joining a rebellion. "Sarah's right. We've sat in the back long enough!" Christina declared.

Rachael stood up, nodding emphatically: "Yeah Mom, it's time to go to Communion."

The elderly and the disabled people turned their ears to our conversation. They smiled as if witnessing something momentous.

I took a deep breath. "OK."

We opened the glass doors and a flood of sunlight beamed down upon us from the skylights. Together, the four of us walked down the church aisle and toward the altar, with Sarah leading the way.

The Communion hymn sounded angelic as many voices sang the verses of "On Eagle's Wings":

> And he will raise you up on eagle's wings
> Bear you on the breath of dawn
> Make you to shine like the sun,
> And hold you in the palm of his hand.

Sarah swayed back and forth, smiling broadly at the parishioners who filled the pews. Christina and Rachael kept whispering to me, "Keep going, Mom. You can do it."

Drawing closer to the altar, I watched my girls receive Communion. Just before Sarah received the Host, she bowed demonstratively. "Body of Christ," the priest said.

"Amen."

I stepped forward, and for a moment, time seemed to stand still. As the Bread was placed in my hands, I had a flashback to Sarah's First Communion and suddenly realized that I had missed something. Though Sarah's life was broken in so many ways, patterned and colored with imperfections, God died for her. With every twirl, she proclaimed and celebrated her faith. Why wouldn't she dance before the Body and Blood? No wonder she curtsied before these signs of extravagant, over-the-top love.

"Body of Christ" the priest said.

"Amen" I replied.

I took a big swig from the cup and felt God touch my spirit. The God who became human and Bread, the God who died and rose from the dead, the God who understands what it means to be human and breakable. That God was with me and Don and the kids and everyone who was gathered that day for Mass.

"God loves us," I told myself.

In that moment, my spirit twirled.

* * *

Thanks to Sarah, I look at the Eucharist now much differently than when I was young. Each Sunday, when you and I come to the altar of the Lord, something momentous happens. As baptized believers, we stand before the panes of God's story. There, in the reflection of his Body and Blood, our sufferings are seamed to his. "By his wounds you have been healed" (1 Pt 2:24).

For our family, the healing may seem less than perfect because Don and I are still divorced. Like so many broken families, our healing has come slowly and in unusual ways, which I'll share more about shortly. For now, I will say that I still sit in the back of the church. I like being near those who have disabilities. Amid the wheelchairs and canes, I feel close to my humble God and I know that Sarah is worshiping with me from heaven. I also have a great view of the beautiful Catholics who are gathered in the pews before me. Even though we may not always know one another, I feel a special bond with them. Like me, they all have their private stories. When I walk down the aisle toward Communion, I can almost hear the collective prayers of God's people: "Lord, heal me. I'm disabled. I'm financially strapped. I'm grieving. I'm unhappily married. I'm sick. I'm divorced. I'm a sinner in need of grace."

When we come to the Eucharist, we all have a place in the greatest love story of all.

In God's eyes, we are beautiful to behold.

Broken, but blessed.

Chapter 4

Confirmation

Wind Chimes of the Spirit

Only after the intellect has planned
The best and highest, can the ready hand
Take up the brush and try all things received.
—Michelangelo

The Creation of Adam is one of Michelangelo's most famous paintings. The fresco was painted as part of the Sistine Chapel's ceiling somewhere between 1511 and 1512. The masterpiece captures the hand of God reaching out to Adam, the first human.

Most of us are familiar with the fresco. In our modern culture, the image has been reproduced on greeting cards, T-shirts, and murals. A few years back, a close friend gave me a mug imprinted with the sacred image. I call it my holy mug.

Sometimes, when I'm having serious writer's block, I'll fill the mug with tea and stare at the painting on my cup. Lost in thought, I'll pretend I'm at the Vatican, viewing the work of one of the greatest artists of all time.

Adam rests on the right side of the painting. He is young and muscular, a naked figure who seems to be languishing. With his face devoid of any emotion, Adam reaches out to God, his fingers drooping toward his creator.

God, on the other hand, is a grandfatherly figure with a beard. Clothed with a white robe that billows in the wind, his muscles are mighty and defined. As he reaches out to Adam, his index finger is as straight and strong as a current of electricity.

But there's a space that separates Adam from God. Their hands are almost touching but not quite. Some critics have said that the little space holds as much meaning as the magnificent bodies, figures, and colors that define so much of Michelangelo's art.

To some interpreters, that space represents the moment when God touched Adam and breathed life into him.

Have you ever had moment when you felt the touch of God?

I had one of those moments back when the kids were in their late teens. It was a sunny morning in late May. I was sitting on the deck in our backyard, and a soft breeze blew through my hair. Tulips budded in the garden, and the hostas that framed the fence sprouted like green stars. I could smell the fragrance of the red roses that bloomed by the deck. Sarah sat across from me, dressed in a tie-dyed shirt and blue jeans.

As I sipped my tea, I looked around the yard. The day before, we had hosted an end-of-the-year party for Rachael's hockey team. Now, card tables were folded up and leaning against the garage. A garbage can was filled to the brim with empty cans of soda and paper plates.

Around twenty girls had tie-dyed shirts in buckets of water that we had lined up in the basement. After taking their shirts outside and drying them in the sun, they began decorating them with glitter pens and markers.

Rachael's teammates often spent time at our home. They knew Sarah well, accepted her disability, and in a way, had become our second family. The girls had insisted that Sarah come to the party, and now they were gathered around her, helping her make a shirt. "Sarah, let's put a crown on the front." "Do you want to use gold glitter or pink?" "It's gonna turn out awesome!" came the chorus of adolescent voices.

I watched from the deck as Rachael penned the words "Princess Sarah" on the sleeve.

"It's-it's beeeutiful," Sarah squealed, clapping her hands in delight.

Rachael was a junior in high school, a bubbly, freckled-faced girl who always wore her hair in a ponytail. She was the youngest of our three daughters. By rite of her birth order, she should've been the child who received a disproportionate amount of attention, the coddled child. But Sarah had always taken center stage, her disabilities requiring Rachael to become a little parent of sorts, Sarah's protector and guide.

Unlike our feisty Christina, Rachael had a quietness about her and always deferred her own achievements to Sarah's many needs. An accomplished athlete, Rachael had been voted the most valuable player by her hockey team and was the goalie for the girls' soccer team. She had won many prestigious awards and excelled in the honors program at her school. She dated nice boys, went shopping at the mall, and talked on the phone for hours. Sometimes, late at night, I'd notice her reading the Bible in her room.

I was always a little worried that Rachael wasn't receiving the praise she deserved. Don and I could always count on her to be responsible and admired her humility and kindness. Now, as the team ate hotdogs and chips, Sarah held her glittering shirt up to the sun. In that moment, I pulled Rachael aside. "I'm so proud of who you are becoming," I whispered.

My youngest daughter hugged me. Then, raising her eyebrows as if the conversation was getting way too heavy for a picnic, she said, "Mom, I don't need to be the center of attention. You know that, right? "

* * *

Now that the party was over, Rachael was sleeping in.

"It-it-it was fun yesterday," Sarah said, giggling.

I smiled. "It was," I said as my thoughts turned to the future. Rachael would be leaving for college in a year, and Christina was already away at school. Letters of interest had arrived from out of state colleges addressed to Rachael. "We have a great hockey program for women" one coach had written.

Our three daughters were maturing at a pace we couldn't slow down. Don and I often talked about the girls' futures, especially Sarah's. Unlike her two younger sisters, she would always remain like a child, totally dependent on us. Would we still be caring for Sarah in our old age? Should we start looking at group homes? Was it time to sit down and talk with Christina and Rachael about the "what ifs"? These questions often gave me pause.

I think all parents of disabled children have moments when they fear the future. Our yes to life requires us to constantly advocate for our kids. In Sarah's case, her health was always in the back of our minds. Given her serious heart condition, she could live two more years or twelve. We just didn't know.

I turned my glance toward Sarah. Everything about her sparkled, especially her slanted eyes and bright countenance. *We've learned so much from her,* I told myself.

Sarah opened a notebook and began penning her thoughts on paper. She often wrote us daily quotes, taping them to the bathroom mirror, the kitchen table, or the dashboard of our car. She wrote things such as, "Be Hapy," "Folow yr dreems," and my favorite, "You are the bst mom I evr had in my life."

I took a peek at her thought for the day. It read, "Love is with my hart and I will alwaze bee with God by following it."

"That's beautiful," I told her.

"I-I know, Mom."

Sarah's theology was so much simpler than mine.
God lived within her heart and loved her. Growing
up Catholic, I don't remember being taught that God
loved me, at least not intentionally. Like all my siblings,
I received the sacraments of Baptism, Reconciliation,
Eucharist, and Confirmation one right after the other
like items on a to-do list.

On the day of my Confirmation, the bishop processed down the aisle of our church wearing red vestments. The color red was everywhere: on banners, altar
cloths, and programs. Even the flowers on the altar were
red, vases filled with chrism roses. Hemmed in by other
Catholic classmates in a pew, the grand liturgy began
with extravagant hymns and litanies. Wearing a white
dress with a pink sash, I had spent two years preparing
to receive the sacrament of the "Holy Ghost."

The time of preparation had felt like boot camp.
Well-trained generals, the nuns who imparted the faith
equipped us for spiritual battle. Dressed in full habit,
they wore their coat of arms. Their crisp black veils,
stiffened from starch, helmeted their heads; their silver crosses looked like shields; and their black tunics,
pleated to the ground, marked them as warriors for
Christ. Every Wednesday evening, they reminded us
that the sacrament would make us soldiers of Christ.
"Confirmed Catholics are obligated to defend the faith
by word and deed," we were told.

We learned that during rule of the Roman Empire,
Christians were routinely tortured to death for their
beliefs. With wide eyes, I listened to stories of martyrs

who had been beaten and beheaded, burned alive at the stake, or thrown into the sea with an anchor.

"Sometimes following Christ requires great sacrifice," the nuns admonished.

As ninth graders, we were no longer babes in the arms of our parents. "You've come of age," the nuns said. Though we had once been cradled at the font and our parents had promised to bring us up in the faith, things were different now.

"It's your time to say yes. Will you follow Christ?" the holy sisters asked.

I remembered feeling the weight of that decision. Did I really want to be a soldier for Christ? I was barely fourteen years old! Was I ready to sacrifice my life to the Lord? For weeks, we studied the seven gifts of the Spirit: wisdom, understanding, counsel, knowledge, fortitude, piety, and fear of the Lord. I resonated with one gift more than all the others: fear of the Lord.

Back then, I wrongly assumed that being afraid of God was a good thing.

* * *

When the day of my Confirmation finally arrived, the bishop gave me a soft slap on my cheek. *Will I be called to suffer?* Only God knew how my journey of faith would unfold.

As my forehead was anointed with oil, the fragrance of chrism was so strong my eyes began to water. "I anoint you with the Sign of the Cross, and I confirm you with the chrism of salvation, in the name of the Father, and of the Son, and of the Holy Ghost" the bishop said.

Walking back to my pew with hands folded, I felt all of my fingers begin to shake. Of my own free will, I had said yes to God. I was now a confirmed soldier of Christ.

Sarah had never gone through the Confirmation process, unlike our other daughters. When she was a ninth grader, she was still functioning at the level of a first grader. At that time, Don and I were hesitant to enroll her in the Confirmation program at our parish. Like so many parents of disabled kids, we faced a holy dilemma: Should we prepare our daughter for a sacrament that required a level of maturity and intellect that she didn't possess? Was she obligated to study the teachings of the Church when her delight was writing misspelled notes and reading fairy tales? Or should we trust that the Holy Spirit had ways of compensating for the lone chromosome that caused her disability?

The breeze rustled through the trees, causing leaves to flap in the wind like hands applauding. The wind chimes by the garage clinked, reminding me of the triangles I once played in kindergarten. Sarah reached out for my hand and covered it with hers.

Above us, below us, over us, in us a blessed presence billowed.

I looked at Sarah's face, marked with all the telltale signs of disability. Her eyes were filled with sunlight. She looked at me as if to say, *Yes Lord, I accept the imperfections of my appearance, my heart condition, my speech impediment, and my cognitive deficiencies. Yes, I will follow you and offer my sufferings for the kingdom of God. Yes, I will show others who you are by loving them as you have loved me.*

The wind fluttered through the rose bushes, and a few red petals fall to the ground. We were in a sacred space, and God was touching us. With Sarah's hand still on mine, I reread her quote for the day: "Love is with my hart and I will alwaze bee with God by following it."

Sarah's inscription was much more than a scribbled note. It was a Confirmation of the faith she possessed. On this day of wind and red petals, she had come of age. Of her own free will, moved by Spirit, she was proclaiming, "I will follow you Lord."

Up until that moment, I had been content to follow the prescribed rules of the Church as a dutiful soldier. My faith had called me to serve and care for my family in ways that required great stamina and energy. In raising my children, one with special needs, I had gotten used to my duties and was always in-step for the next assigment. I was fighting the battles that all parents of special needs children fight: exhaustion, uncertainty, and sometimes even despair.

But as I sat with Sarah on the deck, I took a deep breath and inhaled the wind of the spirit. *Love is with my hart.* In the quietness, I realized I was battleworn. I was languishing about the future, my fingers drooping toward the Lord. *What was to become of our family?*

"Even good soldiers must rest" came the command of the Holy Spirit.

In the sacred space of our backyard, in that little pocket of space between heaven and earth, I handed my helmet to God. Closing my eyes, I took a deep breath. *Perhaps the Holy Spirit needs something more from me than my service.*

I called to mind these encouraging words: "Consider the lilies of the field, how they grow; they neither toil nor spin, yet I tell you, even Solomon in all his glory was not clothed like one of these. But if God so clothes the grass of the field, which today is alive and tomorrow is thrown into the oven, will he not much more clothe you—you of little faith?" (Mt 6:28–30).

In that moment, I did nothing but trust. And my spirit was revived.

As confirmed Catholics, we are all warriors, called to lay down our lives for God and others. But we are no use to God if we are tired or afraid of what lies ahead. The fear of the Lord is an invitation to rest in the quiet awesomeness of God. Sarah taught me this.

Tomorrow, you and I will don our battlegear. The good fight of faith will be fought and we will serve valiantly. But not today. Today is a time to rest in the spirit, to breathe in the beauty of the present, and to recieve the touch of God.

Chapter 5

Marriage

Here Comes the Bride

And now faith, hope, and love abide, these three;
and the greatest of these is love.

—1 Corinthians 13:13

I was planting lilies in my backyard when Bennett
came through the back gate. Wearing a Wisconsin
sweatshirt and blue jeans, he carried two lattes from
a local coffee shop.

"What brings you here on this sunny Tuesday?" I
asked, greeting him with a wave.

Christina had begun dating this tall young man
just a few months earlier, right about the time I moved
into the small home I now called my "cottage." Setting
my shovel aside, we sat down at my picnic table and
Bennett began talking about Christina. "She's so spar-
kly," he beamed.

When he pulled out a small box, I put my hand over my mouth. I knew what was inside. Unbeknownst to me, he had already talked to Don and Rachael. Now, it was my turn to give my approval.

"May I marry Christina?" he asked.

There were no words to describe my joy. From the first moment I met Bennett, I knew he was perfect for Christina. Like my daughter, he was a social worker who had a special fondness for those with special needs. A cancer survivor, he had gone through chemo treatment in his teens. Now in his late twenties he was cancer-free, but that experience had deepened his faith and given him a maturity of spirit rarely found in someone so young. He understood the challenges Christina had lived through and wanted to be part of her story.

Bennett waited for my answer. I could feel tears falling down my cheeks, plopping onto the picnic table like raindrops.

"Is that a yes?" he asked.

I jumped up and hugged him as tightly as I could. "Yes! Yes!" I exclaimed. I simply couldn't express what I felt in that moment. Bennett's announcement made me feel as if I had won the Publishers Clearing House sweepstakes. Don and I had always wanted a son. "Welcome to the family!"

We held up our two lattes like glasses of champagne. "To happiness," we toasted.

The following spring, I hosted a wedding shower at my cottage. The weather forecasters had promised a picture perfect day: seventy degrees and sunny. At around 8 a.m., my five sisters arrived, each of them carrying a variety of supplies to help me prepare for an authentic English tea. Like worker bees, my elder sisters began setting up tables in the backyard, adorning them with white linens and fine china. Meanwhile, my younger sisters prepared cucumber sandwiches and scones in the kitchen.

Amid the bustle, my youngest sister, Annie, and I began ironing an assortment of wedding gowns from the past. With the living room windows open, the summer breeze blew softly through the room. Decades earlier, the timeworn dresses had been worn by Christina's grand-mothers and aunts. Most of them were now yellowed with age. My dress, too, was in the mix.

A few days before, Annie and I had planned a game called "Can You Guess Who Wore the Dress?" Now, as we hung the dresses around the fireplace, we found ourselves doubling over with laughter.

"Can you believe we actually walked down the aisle in these?" I asked.

"What were we thinking?" Annie replied.

In the early 1980s, my sisters and I were married like dominos, one right after the other. At that time, wed-ding fashion was influenced by the gown Princess Diana had worn when she married Prince Charles in 1981. Her marriage ceremony had been televised across the world, and the commentators said her silk taffeta dress was hand-embroidered with 10,000 pearls. The lace train that followed her down the aisle of St. Paul's Cathedral was more than twenty-five feet long.

Like many other brides, I chose a wedding gown with enormously puffy sleeves, just like Diana's. Now, so many years later, the sleeves on my wedding dress looked like they were filled with helium and my long veil lay rumpled over the ironing board like a bolt of lace.

After Annie ironed my dress, she held it up to the sunlight. "It's a miracle," she murmured. My gown was in pristine condition, as white as the day I wore it years ago.

Staring at the dress, memories of my wedding day began to surface. Don and I stood together on an altar decorated with vibrant banners and vases filled with multicolored flowers. Like my wedding gown, Don's tuxedo was an unbroken splash of white from his jacket to his shoes.

Our wedding theme was gleaned from the ninth chapter of Genesis. In our mid-twenties, we listened to the first reading: "I have set my bow in the clouds, and it shall be a sign of the covenant between me and the earth. Whenever I bring clouds over the earth and the bow is seen in the clouds, I will remember my covenant that is between me and you and every living creature of all flesh; and the waters shall never again become a flood to destroy all flesh. When the bow is in the clouds, I will see it and remember the everlasting covenant between God and every living creature of all flesh that is on the earth" (Gn 9:13–16).

In so many ways, it was a prophetic reading. In the coming years, Don and I would face a flood of unexpected challenges. Like every marriage, the rains of uncertainty would fall and hurricanes would come. But on this day of celebration, there were no foreboding storms in sight. As we stood in the presence of God and the community, we exchanged our vows: "I promise to be true to you in good times and in bad, in sickness and in health. I will love you and honor you all the days of my life."

We were too young to comprehend the mystery we were entering into, the awesome and sometimes confusing mystery outlined so beautifully in the *Catechism of the Catholic Church*: "Since God created him man and woman, their mutual love becomes an image of the absolute and unfailing love with which God loves man. It is good, very good, in the Creator's eyes" (*CCC*, 1604).

Our relationship, for better or worse, was a sign of Christ's never-ending love for us. Come what may, God's love would always arch over our lives.

As we exchanged our rings, the priest said, "May the Lord bless these rings which you are giving to each other as a sign of your love and fidelity."

Just as our rings had no beginning or end, we were agreeing to love and care for each other for a lifetime. More important, we were entering into a covenant with God and God with us.

Covenant. The word means "a formal and serious agreement or promise." A few years later, God allowed us to cradle a sign of the covenant in our arms; two more signs came in the following years. By their very existence, our children gave testimony to the permanence of God's love for our family. Created in the image and likeness of God, our girls were three distinct crayons sent to leave their colorful mark in the world. Christina was responsible and smart, a natural caretaker who had an innate sense of justice, even at an early age. Rachael was a gifted athlete with never ending energy, kindhearted, and always on the move. Sarah was the family sage, our wise counselor and guide.

Our children were wedding gifts from God. In them, we could see, hear, and feel the beauty of heaven. Many Catholic parents have moments when they realize the power of God's love at work in their marriage. Certainly that was true for us. Sometimes, as our little girls slept in their beds, we would look at them and try to formulate prayers of thanksgiving. Usually no words came, just feelings of humility as we beheld the handiwork of God.

Yet, like so many marriages, our relationship was clouded with financial stress, disability, sickness, and damage from the past that seemed irreparable. Neither of us knew that we were bringing our past hurts into our relationship, two tightly packed suitcases whose contents only damaged our marriage further.

We did everything to salvage our relationship. We prayed. We sought counseling. We tried to pretend that our hurts didn't hurt, but the turning point came when Don and I realized that our children were watching us gasp for breath. Our beloved daughters were innocent bystanders, signs and symbols of grace. Though we struggled to stabilize our boat, we capsized in the waters of divorce.

The girls were in their teens when Don and I separated. While we signed divorce decrees and divided our assets, we did our best to shield our children from what remained of the storms. In the midst of the downpour, I kept hearing that passage from the First Letter to the Corinthians, "And now faith, hope, and love abide, these three; and the greatest of these is love" (13:13).

The scriptures tell us that God hates divorce (see Mal 2:16). I can understand why. Why would a God, who calls himself love, find pleasure in the dissolution of marital love? Many Catholics, I'm sure, have quietly struggled with this same question. A close friend once told me that her divorce was worse than death. How true this is for many of us. When someone dies, the faith community comes together to share the loss. A Mass is offered for the deceased. Usually, there is a funeral luncheon and a burial at the cemetery, both of which help bring closure. In the shadow of a casket, hugs, tears, and words of consolation can be shared.

But more often than not, divorcées must grieve quietly. There is no funeral to mark this very complex and private loss. Perhaps this is because marriage, by definition, is intimate. When two people make a commitment to love each other for life, the unraveling of that love is a family affair, not an announcement to be read at an assembly. The hurts and heartaches of a divorced couple can fall only under the protection of God's hand.

But here's what I've learned about divorce: God's fidelity toward a broken family remains immutable. His covenant endures, even when divorce papers are signed and sealed. Sarah, our wise sage, imparted these important truths.

* * *

A couple of years after our divorce, Sarah found my wedding dress in a storage box in the basement.

"Mom, can I-I-I try it on?" she asked.

"Of course," I answered.

As we fluffed out the long train, I helped her adjust the oversized sleeves. When she tried on the veil, she smiled: "I-I feel like a bride."

"You are," I replied, smoothing out the lace.

By that time she was a young lady, short of stature but tall in wisdom. She understood that the gown of a bride was symbolic. Most of her beloved fairy tales ended with a wedding of some sort, and in Sarah's mind, love and marriage were magical. She believed that real love could turn a frog into prince or a swan into a princess. Even a beast, blessed with a kiss, could be transformed into a beautiful creation.

When I tried to zip my gown over Sarah's pudgy waistline, the zipper got stuck and we both started laughing. "It's-it's just a little bit tight." Sarah said, giggling. No matter. Sarah's face beamed as she stood before a full length mirror hanging on the basement wall. As she smiled, her eyes closed, a sign that her joy was uncontainable.

When Christina and Rachael arrived home from school, they came down the stairs, curious about what was happening in the basement. "Sarah, you look beautiful," the two said in unison, and Sarah curtsied, her fluffy gown rustling.

In the weeks that followed, the gown would be Sarah's uniform. Sometimes she would sit on a camel back chair in our living room, paging through old magazines filled with photos of Princess Diana on her wedding day. I thought she looked like the host of Masterpiece

Theatre, sitting so proud and portly with such a stately presence in layers of white.

One day I saw her sitting on her bed with my veil trailing over her shoulders. That day, she was reading a little red Bible she had received for her birthday. On the front, she had written the words "The Princess Bible" with a colored marker. Though she couldn't read very well, she ran her finger over the sacred scriptures as though she were taking in every word.

My veil had become her prayer shawl. She was God's princess, the beloved bride of her heavenly prince. It was as if the Lord was saying to her, his bride, "I have loved you with an everlasting love" (Jer 31:3).

Sarah knew the God of love far better than I did. So many times, I wondered if God loved me at all; I had failed in so many ways. But Sarah never seemed to doubt God's faithfulness. That day, as she held her Bible, I wondered if she was praying for our family. Maybe the unspoken words of her spirit were reaching the ears of her heavenly groom. I longed to know God in the same way she did.

The solace of that moment didn't last very long. About an hour later, while sweeping the hallway outside Sarah's room, I heard her open a can of diet soda.

Pop.

Crack.

Swishhhhhhhhhhh.

Clutching my broom, I saw the soda spray over my wedding dress. My gown was splattered with soda, and she hung her head in dismay.

"S-s-s-sorry, Mom."

"It's OK, Sarah." As horrified as I was by the stains I saw spreading across my dress, how could I reprimand this young bride who now smelled like Diet Coke? I immediately tossed the dress in the washing machine, but the stains never came out. Nonetheless, Sarah continued to wear the blemished gown, happily, until the day she went home to God.

Now I watched Annie hang that same dress by the fireplace. Earlier that week, I had watched a commercial for one of those products promising to whiten and brighten even the toughest cases. On a whim, I had soaked my dress in the waters of the miraculous cleaner. Much to my and Annie's surprise, every spot of soda along with all the other signs of Sarah's dedicated love for that dress had disappeared—just in time for the wedding shower.

My backyard now looked like an authentic English garden, complete with flowers, polished china, and teapots. Christina and Rachael had just arrived, and both were dressed in an antique hats and dresses. The two of them waved to me in unison. "Hi, Mom!" they called out.

As I stood there, I thought about the small healings that had come to our family since Sarah's death eight years earlier. Slowly but surely, Don and I were becoming friends again. Though we were still legally divorced and still working through our issues, the experience of losing Sarah had transformed us. During that journey of deepest mourning, we found comfort in sharing our memories of Sarah and expressed our concern for our other daughters. In those moments, we had climbed into the same boat of grief, the two of us drifting side by side through our sea of indescribable sadness.

Neither of us had pursued the annulment process, probably because the family we created together, for better or worse, was something we could still see, hear, and feel. Rowing with broken paddles, Don and I were now moving forward together. The rains had stopped, and glints of sunlight pierced through the clouds.

Strangely, gradually, our grief had given us a stronger sense of God's permanence in our relationship. During the months of mourning, I had gotten into a routine of bringing Don meals and helping him clean his home. At times when money had gotten tight, Don graciously helped me with funds. As a family, we were now having dinner together at my home not every Sunday but often enough to call it a regular thing.

Just a week earlier, we had gathered in my backyard for a family picnic. While Don grilled brats, he and Bennett bantered about the Green Bay Packers and Minnesota Vikings, the two of them debating about which team would make it to the Super Bowl. "The Packers will go all the way," Bennett said. "I don't know; the Vikes are pretty good this year," Don replied.

Meanwhile, the girls and I drank Diet Coke and paged through wedding magazines. As we talked about Christina's big day, I showed them my "mother of the bride" dress, a classic pink silk dress with a sash. "Mom, you should *so* wear your hair in an updo!" they advised.

Out of all the young men Christina could've chosen for her husband, she choose someone that both Don and I adored, one more sign of God's unending covenant to our family. In the years to come, Rachael would probably get married, too, and maybe there would be grandchildren. Just the thought of cradling a new baby brought me joy.

The aroma of scones filled my home, and I couldn't help but think of how Sarah would have loved this party, all of these dresses and all of this joy. She would have loved Bennett, too.

As I looked at my wedding dress, now draped over the fireplace, a passage from Isaiah came to mind: "Come now, let us argue it out, says the Lord: though your sins are like scarlet, they shall be like snow; though they are red like crimson, they shall become like wool" (1:18).

In September, Christina and Bennett were married. Christina wore a simple gown tinged with a hint of blush as Don and I escorted her down the aisle together, our arms linked to hers in an unbreakable chain. Her presence was like a bell, softly chiming. Rachael stood for her sister to the side of the altar, a lovely, smiling maid of honor in blue silk. Front and center by a cross, waiting for his bride, was Bennett, the handsome prince in a gray tuxedo and bow tie. Somehow, I knew that Sarah was there, too.

As they exchanged vows and rings, they made a covenant to each other, and God made a covenant to them. They were entering into the mystery of God's unfailing love. Don and I were eucharistic ministers, and the two of us cried softly as we shared the sacred Body and Blood with our guests.

God was present, and I was rendered speechless. It was all too beautiful for words.

Though statistics show that many get divorced, they also show that more stay together. The grace of the Holy Spirit comes to married couples in many different ways: through joy and companionship, intimacy and shared love, and humor that always makes the journey more fun. I always smile when I see couples in their eighties and nineties walking hand in hand. They give me hope that it's never too late for healing.

Some families experience God's healing through separation, the annulment process, and the chance to begin anew. The important thing to remember is that our Lord pours out his grace to each family according to his will. We should never judge how God might be working in someone's life because we can never know their story.

As for Don and I, we aren't living out our sacramental vows the way most Catholics do. But our relationship is marked with signs and symbols of God's presence. God holds our future, and we are open to the surprises he might send our way.

One thing we know for sure. There are three things that remain. Faith. Hope. And love. And the greatest of these is love.

Chapter 6

Holy Orders
Couriers of Grace

Our Lord's love makes itself seen quite as much
in the simplest of souls as in the most highly gifted, as long as there is no resistance offered to his
grace.

—St. Thérèse of Lisieux, *Story of a Soul*

U
p until about the age of twelve, Sarah's speech
impediment made it difficult for people to
understand her, especially when she was excited and wanted to share something. This often caused
other parishioners at our church to walk away from her.

Not Fr. Marty. In his late thirties, he was tall and
lanky with wavy hair just beginning to recede. Though
he was only at our parish for a few years, I look back on
his priesthood and smile. Every Sunday morning when
our young family arrived for Mass, he would greet us

with open arms. He'd converse with our daughters as if he were a kid himself: "Did you win your hockey game?" "How did that science fair project go?" "I'll meet you after Mass for doughnuts!" Fr. Marty always made us feel as if the church was another place to call home.

I was especially touched by the way he engaged with Sarah. When she stuttered, he knelt down before her so he could look into her eyes. Sometimes he even raised her chin so that they could make better eye contact.

"Sarah, what's been happening in your life?" he'd ask.

"My birthday is-is coming up!" she'd always say, even though her special day was inevitably months away.

"Mine is too!" Fr. Marty would reply, joyfully slapping his knee. "Don't you just love birthdays, Sarah?"

"Yes-s-s-s-s," Sarah would reply, grinning.

Fr. Marty was a good priest. He would go from his joyful, childlike conversations with my daughter straight to the altar. There we'd watch him preside over the Eucharist *in persona Christi*. God had set him apart, giving him the highest honor of consecrating the bread and wine on behalf of all the everyday Catholics like us who filled the pews. This priestly duty elevated him to a royal status, and yet he didn't seem to look at it that way. Quite the opposite—he was the servant priest.

Given Sarah's fascination with fairy tales, she was mesmerized by Fr. Marty and his vestments: the white chasubles and colorful stoles that draped over his shoulders. Sometimes, she even bowed in his presence. Once Sarah asked me if Fr. Marty was a king.

"Mom, is-is-is his crown invisible?" she asked. I didn't know how to respond. Sarah's concept of the priesthood was so uncomplicated. In her eyes, Fr. Marty was the great ruler of our parish.

Growing up Catholic, I had been taught that the role of an ordained priest was to be the mediator between God and the people, between heaven and earth, "configured" to Christ through the sacrament of Holy Orders and the power of the Holy Spirit. Somewhere in my Catholic upbringing, I had memorized a phrase: *in persona Christi*, which means, "in the person of Christ."

When I was in high school, I attended the ordination of a young deacon who led our youth group. As a teenager, I was awestruck as the candidates for priesthood lay prostrate on the altar, a sign of complete submission and of giving their entire lives to God. After the Litany of the Saints, the candidates knelt before the bishop. A hush fell over the church as the bishop placed his hands on the head of each candidate. There were no verbal prayers offered during this time; the silence was so profound that many people teared up and had to dry their eyes with tissues.

A note in the program explained that the "essential matter" of the sacrament was being "transmitted" to the priest during the laying on of hands. Right before our eyes, the power of the Holy Spirit was poured out on ordinary men, a power first received from Christ and then passed through the apostles and their successors.

This moment of holiness and awe made it seem like suddenly these men had become angels or something. They were different from us, more special, more needed by God. The whole church seemed to feel it.

Years later, on the day of Sarah's Baptism, the priest anointed our baby with chrism and proclaimed, "As Christ was anointed Priest, Prophet, and King, so may you live always as a member of his Body, sharing everlasting life."

These words jarred me. My little daughter, who we already knew would never be as smart, graceful, or athletic as some other children, had an important place in God's kingdom. In Baptism she had become priestly, a "little Christ."

I didn't ponder this much, though, as my daughter required much care and then my next two daughters followed. But as they grew, questions about Holy Orders and the meaning of priesthood mounted within me. In the early 2000s, when my girls were almost teenagers, the national and regional scandals of clergy abuse unfolded after a series of articles were published by *The Boston Globe*. For many months, the details of clergy abuse were broadcast on CNN. While ironing clothes in the living room, I listened to television reports of grown men who had been damaged by priests as young boys. "The Church failed to protect me," one man told a reporter as he stood with his lawyer.

Like other Catholics, I was angry and deeply saddened. I grieved for the victims, their families, and the Church as a whole. I was especially concerned for my own children. One afternoon, breaking news was reported that the Archbishop of Boston had resigned. Christina walked in the door from middle school and overheard the report. "Mom, why didn't that cardinal protect the kids?"

I had no real answer for her. How was I, or any of the ordinary Catholics I knew, to process these revelations? Hadn't the sacrament of Holy Orders set priests apart to lead, guide, nurture, and protect the people of God? And what about those who had been entrusted with deeper responsibilities of leadership—the bishops and the cardinals?

I shut off the news. "I don't really know," I told my daughter. The shining images of the ordination I had attended in my youth were now tainted by the dark secrets of the Church.

I watched as others around me wrestled with the issue of clerical abuse. As I was a faith formation director at a large Catholic church, parishioners would often drop by my office to talk about the nonstop news. "I don't know how to be Catholic anymore," one mother of five confided as we ate lunch. Another parishioner told me he had joined a large nondenominational congregation in the area. "The Catholic Church needs to change," he said. My heart went out to the good priest who was shepherding our congregation well. At one of our staff meetings, his voice cracked with emotion as he spoke of the scandal. "It's been hard," he confessed.

None of us really knew how to handle our conflicting feelings about the priesthood. Most of us had a deep appreciation for the priests who had enriched our journey of faith, baptized our children, anointed our

loved ones, given us the gift of the Eucharist, and pas-
tored us through times of struggle. But a quiet distrust
of the clergy was spreading throughout the Church, a
sickness that couldn't be contained.

One afternoon while on my lunchbreak, I found
myself looking into in a *Catechism* collecting dust in
the parish library. These words caught my attention:
"Christ, high priest and unique mediator, has made of
the Church 'a kingdom, priests for his God and Father.'
The whole community of believers is, as such, priestly.
The faithful exercise their baptismal priesthood through
their participation, each according to his own vocation,
in Christ's mission as priest, prophet, and king. Through
the sacraments of Baptism and Confirmation the faithful are 'consecrated to be . . . a holy priesthood'" (*CCC*,
1546).

There was that teaching again, the same words that
had jarred me years before at Sarah's Baptism. Even if
I wasn't wearing a chasuble or a stole, I had a respon-
sibility to partner with Christ as "priest, prophet, and
king," as did every baptized believer in the Church.
Whether we were ordained priests or everyday believers, we were all part of a holy priesthood. But how was
everyday priesthood different from ordained priesthood? Was the Spirit I received in Baptism different from
the Spirit poured out upon priests in the sacrament of
Holy Orders?

I decided to go to the sacrament of Reconciliation
to seek answers. A trusted colleague recommended a
priest who lived in a small town about an hour and a

half away from my home. "He's in his eighties, a cancer survivor with great wisdom," she told me.

After driving through some back roads in rural Minnesota, I steered into the parking lot of a church built in the early 1900s. When I walked into the confessional, a small room behind the altar, Fr. Joseph was waiting for me. In the light of a dimly lit lamp, I saw a kind face covered with wrinkles. A small man, he seemed almost hidden in a long linen cassock.

"I don't know how to be reconciled to the Church," I told him.

"Hmmmm," he murmured, closing his eyes as if he was seeking guidance from above. In the silence, he reminded me of Yoda, that diminutive character in the *Star Wars* movies. But his smallness could not veil his deep understanding. His very expression opened me up even more.

I spoke of clergy abuse in the news and my anger at the priests who had preyed upon children. "No one was there to save them; why not?" I asked. I shared stories of friends and colleagues who had been victimized by priests when they were young and now found themselves going through intensive counseling. "They still remember the details," I told Fr. Joseph.

As a lay worker in the Church, I was in partnership with other directors of faith formation. Most of us were women, in the trenches each day, following the great commission of Christ to "make disciples" of all children. We taught the little ones the sacraments, shared the Gospel, and served their families. We cherished the kids and mothered them. Our work for the Church was more than just a job. It was our vocation.

Fr. Joseph handed me a tissue, and I heard myself sigh.

"Right now, I could use a good Church," I said, trying to regain my composure. "But our Church is broken."

Again the silence came.

Then, out of the stillness, came the priest's strong voice: "You are called to be a prophet."

A prophet?

What a strange response. I wanted forgiveness, healing, some way to make things right, to think things through, some hope. Not this. Not a challenge.

His eyes met mine, and in his face, I saw the radiance of Christ himself. "Be a witness to truth," he said.

How do I do that?

"Seek the truth in your family. Proclaim the truth to your children. " he went on, and I found myself thinking about my kids. The three of them were growing into such beautiful young women, each of them blessed with a prism of gifts. They weren't perfect, but they were teaching me powerful lessons of faith, forgiveness, and unconditional love. "Sarah has Down syndrome, but she keeps leading me into a deeper relationship with God."

Fr. Joseph listened intently.

"Your children bear the light of truth." he said. "Jesus is the truth; you know this, yes?" I nodded. As I sat in quiet reflection, the clock on the wall ticked softly. "You must live the truth of Christ in your work, your writings, and your service to the children," said

Fr. Joseph. "And pray that I, your servant, may live his truth for you."

My role in the everyday priesthood was clear. I was called to be Christ in the church of my home, family, and work. These were sanctified places and my priestly role was to serve and grow within them. But how was Fr. Joseph's role different from mine?

In the lamplight of the confessional, I remembered a birthday I had celebrated a week earlier. That morning, a truck from a local florist pulled into my driveway. After the delivery man knocked on my door, he handed me a dozen red roses in a vase. "These are so beautiful, but who sent them?" I wondered. Attached to a long ribbon was a card that read *We love you, Mom. Happy Birthday!* The roses had come from my daughters; they had saved their babysitting money to buy them. The deliverer tipped his hat to me: "Have a great day ma'am."

Priests are couriers of grace, I thought. Anointed to serve, they come to the doorstep of our souls, carrying beautiful graces: hope for the faithful, encouragement for the hurting, protection for the vulnerable, strength for the journey.

I looked at Fr. Joseph with new eyes. *Priests are the hired hands of God*, I thought. Their role, unlike mine, was to deliver the sacraments to God's people. *They bear gifts to the faithful.*

In the waters of Baptism, sprinkled by a priest, God signs his name. When a priest anoints a new soldier of Christ, the fragrance of heaven lingers. In bread and wine, God's most beautiful bouquet, the very presence of Christ is passed from the priest's hands to ours.

As my thoughts returned to the Confession I had come to make, I began to say the act of contrition: "Bless me father for I have sinned . . ." After I had asked for forgiveness for my anger at the Church and prayed an act of contrition, Fr. Joseph said, "God can transform anger into hope." With that, he extended his hands over me, gave me absolution, and prayed: "Go in peace and proclaim to the world the wonderful works of God who has brought you salvation."

I imagined the Lord placing his hands upon my head. The power of Fr. Joseph's blessing brought forth a peace and comfort I could not explain. This was mercy in its most mysterious form: God's unstoppable grace flowing to me from a very imperfect and broken Church.

Since that Confession with Fr. Joseph, I have taken his wise counsel to heart. As everyday Catholics, you and I are invited to be the prophets we were anointed to be when we were baptized.

How do we do this?

By being *in persona Christi* in our everyday lives. By sharing the truth of Jesus. By serving our families, changing diapers, driving our kids to soccer practice, giving someone else our parking space, comforting a friend, helping an elderly person, smiling at a stranger, and teaching the children. These daily gifts of love are the sacraments that we, as everyday Catholics, are called to administer. In sharing the truth of Jesus, we, too, become couriers of grace.

Our Church needs healing, and the royal priest-hood of believers must lead the charge. We're going to need good priests like Fr. Marty and Fr. Joseph. And we're going to need our wonderful good nuns, those humble servants who have built our hospitals, schools, orphanages, and domestic shelters, doing so much work even though so often our nuns are forgotten. And we're going to need us, the ordinary prophets devoted to Christ and willing to live his truth.

God's healing will come to our Church if we are open to it. Even priests who abuse their power are not excluded from God's merciful touch. That's the mystery of Holy Orders. The sacraments of God cannot be nul-lified, even if a sinful priest administers them. For the truth is that the essential matter of Holy Orders is the Holy Spirit and the power of the Spirit always presides.

Think of the power of the Holy Spirit and the gifts that empower our Church: wisdom, understanding, counsel, knowledge, fortitude, piety, and fear of the Lord, also known as the gift of wonder. And that's just the beginning! What about love, humor, and laughter? What about patience, encouragement, and forgiveness? The list of gifts is never ending.

Fr. Marty was out of town the week that Sarah died, but he called us on the phone to offer his love and support. "Sarah made me a better priest" he said. He spoke of her joy and simplicity, and the crowns she so often wore. "She lived as a true child of God."

Fr. Marty was a good priest, and Sarah made him a better one. It was the little things about Sarah that made the biggest difference in his priesthood. Filled with joy,

Sarah's smile lit up the world. Despite a significant hearing impairment, she listened well and made others feel heard. Though the lenses of her glasses were thick, she looked into the eyes of others with love and compassion, just like Jesus. Her prayers were always personal, and her words, though stuttered, were wise and joyful. As she had low muscle tone and her steps were measured, she slowed us all down. In doing so, we saw what she saw; the simple wonders of God's creation. These were the things that Fr. Marty spoke of when he said Sarah made him a better priest.

Together, the two of them mirrored the beauty of our Catholic faith. Priest and prophet, crowned with the glory of God—for each other and to the world they proclaimed the truth—*in persona Christi*.

Chapter 7

Anointing of the Sick

The Prince and the Peace

I am not sure exactly what heaven will be like,
but I know that when we die and it comes time
for God to judge us, he will not ask, "How many
good things have you done in your life?" rather
he will ask, "How much love did you put into
what you did?"

—St. Teresa of Calcutta

When I was a teenager, no one in our family knew what to do about my father's alcoholism. In those days, a stigma was attached to family interventions and treatment options. Very few people understood that alcoholism was a disease.

Perhaps if we had known that Dad would die at the age of fifty-nine, we would have been more persistent in trying to help him.

Dad's alcoholism confused us because he wasn't always drinking. Pockets of time each week when Dad was sober allowed us to catch glimpses of who he really was. On weeknights, when he arrived home from work, he would always spend a couple hours with us before retreating to the upstairs den to drink alone. It was just enough time to play a game of Yahtzee at the kitchen table or watch *Wheel of Fortune* in the living room. On Sunday mornings, he would take us to Mass, making sure that every shoe was polished, every veil ironed, and every necktie perfectly straight. On snowy Sunday afternoons, he would skate with us on the ice rink he had built in our backyard.

Back then, there was no organized hockey for girls, but under Dad's watchful eye my sisters and I learned to skate, twirl, and make figure eights. As grown women, we now joke that the six of us could've formed our own hockey team. My brothers, on the other hand, had more opportunities to develop their athletic talents, and my father made sure this happened. When Timmy, Johnny, and Terry were young, he spent hours coaching them in the frigid winds that blew over the backyard ice. With snowbanks piled high around the rink, he demonstrated how to grip a hockey stick and slap-shoot a puck. At both ends of the rink were flimsy nets made from construction cones and sheets. "Ah c'mon, you can do better than that!" my dad would shout when my brothers would miss the net or fall on the ice.

Dad was dramatic, but his heart was quiet and humble. Like so many Minnesota parents, he dreamed that his boys would play in the Minnesota State High School hockey tournament and perhaps receive the college scholarships that would cover tuition he couldn't afford.

Just before we went inside for dinner at the end of these lessons, Dad would sometimes turn his glance upward. Standing in the frozen starlight of Minnesota, his eyes would close just a bit; suddenly the rink became a holy place. When this happened, we would all stand still for a moment, the blades of our skates at rest. "Keep the faith," he would tell us. I was old enough to know that Dad's relationship with God was private but very deep. This nightly proclamation was an evening prayer he recited often.

My brothers went on to play high school hockey, and for five years straight, their team made an appearance at the state tournament. Thousands of people watched them play at a huge arena in Minneapolis. From behind the plexiglass framing the goalpost, my father watched them score goal after goal. The rest of our family cheered from the stands as did many scouts from different colleges. At the end of their high school careers, each of my brothers received a hockey scholarship at Providence College in Rhode Island.

When my younger brother Timmy was a senior at Providence, their hockey team made it to the national championships. I wasn't there, but Timmy often recalls that unforgettable game against Michigan State. In the second period, he scored a goal and looked up to the bleachers where my parents were sitting. Dad was doubled over in a slump, and a chaplain for the team, a Catholic priest, was drawing near. In an instant, the arena became a sacred space. The crowd grew hushed, and out of the pocket of the priest came healing oil.

My mother would later tell me that she couldn't remember what happened during the sacrament. But most likely, when the priest anointed my father, he prayed, "Through this holy anointing may the Lord in his love and mercy help you with the grace of the Holy Spirit. May the Lord who frees you from sin save you and raise you up. Amen" (*CCC*, 1513).

A few hours later, my oldest brother, Johnny, called from Michigan to tell us that Dad had had a fatal heart attack. "Fatal?" I asked. The word rang in my ears. Final. Gone forever. "Dad died?" I could barely believe what I was hearing.

The news hit me hard. Sarah was only three months old at the time, and we had just learned that she needed open heart surgery. I didn't know how to face this unexpected loss. Don and I needed to muster up strength for Sarah's upcoming heart surgery and all the unknowns that her birth had brought. How was I to grieve my father's loss at the same time?

Dad's funeral was held on the Monday of Holy Week. At the wake, my siblings and I talked about how fitting it was that he died watching hockey. "He loved the game," we all agreed. It was so comforting to know that Dad received the sacrament of the Anointing of the Sick in such a strange and unusual way. "I'm so grateful the priest was right there," my mother told us.

A few days later, in the early morning hours of Easter Sunday, I had a dream. My dad came to me in that dream, dressed in a bright yellow sweater and standing in the hallway of our childhood home, outside the dark den where he used to drink cans of Special Export. "Nancy, I'm happy, and I'm finally free," he told me.

Perhaps the Lord was trying say, "Nancy, I was there for your dad in his last moments. Rest assured that healing came to him. Be free as your dad is free." It would take years to understand the meaning of this dream. As time passed and the stories of my own family unfolded, there would be so many moments when I would ask "What if?" or wonder "Maybe if we had . . ."

* * *

Outside the kitchen windows, the snow fell as I ate breakfast with Sarah. Still dressed in her pajamas, Sarah's hair was clipped with sequined barrettes. My other two daughters slept upstairs while the scent of cinnamon toast filled the house.

"Mom, I-I had the most b-e-e-e-utiful dream last night," Sarah said. In the lenses of her glasses, I could see my smiling reflection.

"What did you dream?" I asked.

"I dreamed my-my prince was coming for me." Sarah glowed. From across the table, she reached out and laid her hand on mine.

"Mom, he's coming soon . . . and I-I am so excited."

I felt the familiar softness of her small fingers, all her nails polished pink. Even at twenty-three, she was still so childlike.

A year earlier, I had taken Sarah to the Mayo Clinic for a series of cardiac tests. Sarah had been stopping to catch her breath every time we went grocery shopping. When she danced in our living room, her twirls were becoming sluggish. When she sang her favorite songs, she now whispered the lyrics. She was also taking more naps.

When at last the cardiologist knocked on the door to our examination room, she greeted us warmly and sat down next to us. Dressed in a white coat, she held a clipboard scribbled with notes. Somehow, I knew that our lives were about to change.

"Hello, d-d-doctor," Sarah said as she showed the cardiologist a picture she had just drawn.

"Sarah, I want you to go home today and have a lot of fun with your family. Can you do that?" the doctor loudly asked. That day I had forgotten Sarah's hearing aid so the doctor had to amplify her voice.

"I-I like f-f-fun," Sarah admitted, smiling.

The cardiologist explained that the blood pressure in Sarah's lungs were rising from pulmonary hypertension. "She has a year, perhaps two," the doctor said quietly to me, her eyes holding mine. I was grateful that Sarah couldn't hear our conversation. As we discussed the nonnegotiable realities of this disease, Sarah colored pictures happily.

We always knew that someday Sarah's lung pressure would be compromised, and she had already lived much longer than we had expected. But still, the news felt like a huge tree falling overhead and someone yelling, "TIMBER!"

I turned to Sarah and smiled, trying to pretend that her story wasn't going to have an end. When I stood up, the doctor put down her clipboard and hugged me. "Cherish this time," she instructed me.

"Her life has gone by so fast," I whispered, tears already pooling in my eyes.

As I drove home, Sarah nodded off to sleep in the passenger seat, and I wondered what I was going to do without her. How does a mother begin to say goodbye to a piece of her heart? As a family, how were we to prepare for her death?

When I told Don about Sarah's prognosis, he maintained his composure even as a thin mist filled his eyes. "God has given us this time," he said, broad shoulders rising as he took a deep breath. Christina and Rachael, in contrast, didn't really accept that their sister was dying. "Don't worry, Mom, she will be fine," they told me, almost as if I had imagined the whole thing. In a way, their denial of the truth was a blessing because they didn't pity Sarah or treat her any differently than they always had.

For the most part, nothing changed at all. In the late afternoon, Don would drop by to take Sarah out for dinner as he often did. The girls and I got a kick out of the way Sarah would dress up for her dad like she was going out on date. Sometimes, Christina and Rachael would help her get ready by curling her hair and polishing her nails with glitter. Sarah often wore a pink cardigan that her father had given her, a cashmere sweater trimmed with a sequined cat.

"How do I-I look?" Sarah asked as she stood before a mirror, ruby red lipstick smudged around her grin.

"What a babe!" Christina enthused as she adjusted the tiara on Sarah's head.

When Rachael clipped fake diamonds onto Sarah's ears, she would giggle and raise her hands in the air as if she had just finished a performance on stage. "Ta-da!" she would call out.

After one of these evenings when Don brought Sarah home, she fell asleep on our living room couch. "I'm just a-a little bit tired," she told us.

As Don pulled a blanket over her shoulders, he looked at me: "This is brutal, Nance."

"It really is" was my only answer. I felt worn, and my emotions were wrung out.

Later that night, I sat at the kitchen table and buried my head in my hands. I told myself that it was probably time to have a priest anoint Sarah, but I wondered if Sarah even understood how serious her illness was. We hadn't really talked to her about death, mainly because we didn't know how to. Given her vivid imagination, her understanding of death came from Snow White, the story of the mythical maiden who fell into a deep sleep only to be awakened by her handsome prince.

When it came to the sacrament of the Anointing of the Sick, how were we to explain the difference between spiritual and physical healing to Sarah and the sacred role of oil, priestly prayers, and the laying on of hands? She was still functioning as a child, and a very vulnerable one at that. Having worked in the Church for many years, I knew that Sarah's ability to reason was an important part of the sacrament.

According to the introduction to the Rite of Anointing, "Sick children are to be anointed if they have sufficient use of reason to be strengthened by this sacrament. . . . The faithful should be educated to ask for the sacrament of anointing, and, as soon as the right time comes, to receive it with full faith and devotion. They should not follow the wrongful practice of delaying the reception of the sacrament" (*Pastoral Care of the Sick: Rites of Anointing and Viaticum*, 32). My question remained: Was Sarah able to reason that she would soon leave this world and that a sacred anointing would strengthen and prepare her for the journey to heaven?

As a kid, I had been taught that this sacrament was once called Extreme Unction, meaning "final anointing," and only those who were near the point of death were encouraged to receive it. Only when the Second Vatican Council renamed it Anointing of the Sick did many lay Catholics begin to understand that the role of the sacrament was to offer healing and comfort not only to the dying but also to those who were ill.

I knew that the sacrament wasn't a magic ticket to eternity, and I never doubted that Sarah's salvation was secure. "She's already so close to heaven," I thought. But deep down, I knew that there was another reason I was avoiding the sacrament: I was reluctant to face the truth that she was really going to die. My father had received the sacrament in the very last moments of his life, and I had never gotten to say goodbye. I couldn't get past the idea that this was the "final" sacrament.

The fact that Sarah was always tired only encouraged me to stall. Most anointings were held in the evenings at our church, and she was usually asleep by 7 p.m.

I had to admit, too, that my prayers for Sarah's healing were laced with a deep-seated anger toward God. Even though the Lord had the power to heal Sarah, he was choosing not to. Many unresolved feelings about my father's life and death were triggered by Sarah's life-ending illness. "Lord, you never healed my dad," I accused.

I think Sarah was aware that God and I were battling. As I helped her into bed one night, she confessed, "Mom . . . I-I-I don't want to die."

Like all of us who struggle with our own mortality, Sarah understood that her body didn't work like it used to, that she slept a lot more, and that one day she would go to sleep forever, just like Snow White. She was trying to process what this might mean, reasoning that death was going to be hard, scary, and sad.

I reached out and traced the Sign of the Cross of her forehead. In my mind's eye, I saw myself cradling her as a baby at the baptismal font, and I remembered the priest anointing her with oil and the words he once prayed: "This child of yours has been enlightened by Christ. She is to walk always as a child of the light. May she keep the flame of faith alive in her heart. When the Lord comes, may she go out to meet him with all the saints in the heavenly kingdom."

"Sarah, you are going to a beautiful kingdom," I told her, stroking her hair.

"Yes-s-s-s," she sighed as her face became transfigured with the light of hope.

Images from the scriptures filled my mind. "In the kingdom of heaven, there are streets of gold," I told her.

Sarah's eyes grew wide. "Wow, Mom!"

I felt a surge of courage, as if an angel with a wide wingspan towered over us in protection.

"And Sarah, you can dance on those streets of gold whenever you want, and there's singing in heaven, and everyone will be wearing crowns, just like you. And the best part, when you get to the kingdom, Prince Jesus will have a special banquet prepared for you," I said. We rested in the stillness of the Holy Spirit.

"Mom, I-I can't wait to-to see my prince," she said, a little mischievous glee in her eyes.

Then, Sarah turned to me and began tracing the Sign of the Cross on my forehead. "In-in-in the name of the Fadder, Son, and-and Holy Spirit," she prayed softly. *Amen.*

This moment with Sarah was one of the most transformative moments in my journey of faith. It wasn't the sacrament of the Anointing of the Sick; there was no priest, no oil, and no formal prayers of healing. And yet, it was sacramental. God touched us, comforting us in a way we could receive. Sign and symbol. Grace. God present in our lives.

I kissed her goodnight, and she fell asleep with a smile on her face. She never spoke of her fear of death again. In fact, she began dreaming about heaven and often told me how excited she was to go to the kingdom.

A few weeks later, our family kept a close vigil around her bedside. We were at St. Joseph's Hospital on a snowy evening in January, just one floor above the maternity ward where Sarah was born. It was one of the few times she was hospitalized in her life, and for that we will always be grateful.

"Nance, I'll stay with Sarah tonight. Go home and rest," Don said.

I kissed Sarah goodnight. "Love you," I told her. She smiled. "Love you-you, too, Mom."

She seemed stable, and the girls were tired and needed to sleep at home. The next morning, I got up at around 4 a.m. After bundling up in a down jacket and heavy boots, I took a long walk through our snow-covered neighborhood. It was about twenty degrees below zero as I looked up at the morning sky lit with bright stars.

"Lord, I know Sarah isn't coming back home to our house," I said through tears. I opened my shivering hands and felt the wind blow through my mittens. "Will you take her home to your house?" I prayed.

In the ice, wind, and cold, I drew near to the brightness of God. I knew that I was standing on holy ground, in the presence of the great "I AM," the one who calls himself light. In the warmth, I heard myself saying the same two words over and over again and again: "Thank you."

I simply couldn't stop thanking God for the gift of Sarah's life. For the baptism of blessings that flowed from her life, for the lessons of forgiveness she imparted, for the spirit that fluttered through her stuttered words, for the covenants she called us to live and honor, for the priests she taught, and the host of everyday people she touched, and for the great healing and acceptance I now felt.

"Amen," I whispered as my breath froze in the wind.

When I came in from my winter walk, my cell phone was ringing.

It was the nurse from St. Joseph's Hospital. Sarah had passed away at the exact time I had been offering thanks for the gift of her life.

After driving through freeways covered with snow and ice, the girls and I arrived at the hospital about 5 a.m. Don waited for us at Sarah's bedside, holding her hand. "She's gone," he said—his voice soft and low, his eyes barely open.

I sat down next to Don and laid my head on his shoulder while Christina and Rachael held each other tightly. Looking back now, it seems altogether fitting that Don was there at the end. I carried Sarah into this world, but it was Don who escorted her to the arms of God.

The priest arrived a few minutes later began reading prayers of commendation from a leather breviary:

> All-powerful and merciful God,
> we commend to you Sarah, your servant.
> In your mercy and love,
> blot out the sins

she has committed through human
weakness—

In a loud and feisty voice, Christina interrupted:
"Father, you don't understand; Sarah didn't have any
sins!"

Don and I looked at each other and chuckled under
our breath. Rachael shrugged her shoulders and smiled
through her tears. "She did sneak treats," I said. With
that, we all began laughing.

It was an awkward moment for the priest, I'm sure.
But like a co-conspirator, he joined in the smiling. "I
guess this is a special case," he said, "but everyone can
use some prayers, don't you think?"

As we prayed for Sarah's soul and strength for the
days, months, and years ahead, I kept thinking, "She
was a special case." From her Baptism, she had kept the
flame of faith alive in her heart and shared her sparkle.
Her light had transfigured our lives.

Years later, I've now learned to manage my grief,
though I doubt there will ever come a day when I don't
miss Sarah. Yet I am comforted. The worst of my grief
has been replaced with hope. In her last days, I watched
her bravely move from her fear of death to a joyful
expectation of heaven. She never received the sacrament of the Anointing of the Sick, but I don't think she
needed it. She was well acquainted with her heavenly
prince, and it's easy for me to imagine her dancing in
the kingdom of joy.

As I reverently sift through her life story as I write,
I take time to honor the lessons she taught us. This

unusual princess introduced us to her prince, the God who crowns each of us with peace. There was no guilt in surrendering Sarah to God, just gratefulness for her life alongside the beautiful yet excruciating pain that comes with saying goodbye. I will forever cherish her story.

It's strange, but as I grieved for Sarah, I found myself grieving anew for my father. As I thought about his struggle with alcoholism, I often scolded myself, thinking, *Maybe Dad would've lived longer if we had been more proactive.*

One quiet afternoon, I found myself reading one of the misspelled quotes that Sarah had left behind: "Love is with my hart."

It was a turning point in my grief because I realized I didn't want to carry guilt any longer. I wanted to live as Sarah lived. I wanted to spend the rest of my days on earth adorned with freedom, happiness, and hope. I wanted to let go of everything that veiled the light of Christ in my heart. As I continued to thank God for the gift of Sarah's life, I found myself doing the same thing with Dad. *Thank you for my father's quiet faith. Thank you for his love of family. Thank you for his story.* Filled with gratitude for my father's life, my guilt began to fade and I gradually felt lighter.

I still have days when I wish that death wasn't so incredibly hard. For most of us, grief lessens over time, but we carry our pain for a lifetime. What brings me comfort now is knowing that both Sarah and Dad lived their lives admirably. At the end of their days, God prepared each of them, in a different way, for his kingdom.

Dad received an anointing at a hockey game from a priest. The sacrament of healing was there for him at the hour of death, God's presence in oil and sign. But what's so beautiful about this sacrament is that we don't need to be near death to receive it. If we are sick, despairing, scared, or even if we long to achieve victory over an addiction, this sacrament is meant for us. When the priest, marking us with oil, traces the Sign of the Cross on our foreheads, we can trust that we are not alone. Our prince is near, and his promise is peace. Looking back now, an anointing such as this would've given me strength to care for Sarah in her illness and in those demanding days of early grief.

Yet I am at peace. Sarah's send-off to heaven had its own sacramentality. That night, as we traced crosses on our foreheads, her Baptism was quietly affirmed and our family story celebrated.

Love was the essential element. Cherished child of light. Sign and symbol. God's presence in our life.

Epilogue
Has Anyone Seen God?

I once saw a plaque that read, "Sometimes it's the smallest things that take up the most room in our hearts." Most of us know how true these words are. Over the decades of our lives, we save our favorite memories like treasures. Even though my kids are grown, I store their childhood artwork in a closet by the front door: tiny handprints in plaster, butterflies made of Popsicle sticks, and misspelled cards and letters. I've often told myself that if there was ever a fire, I'd rush to that closet and retrieve as much as possible. I've discovered, as perhaps you have, that small gifts of love are more precious than extravagant possessions.

Mary, the mother of Christ, knew the value of small gifts. In a humble stable—as she cradled her baby, Joseph looked on, the shepherds drew near, and the star above the manger twinkled brightly—we are told that she "treasured all these words and pondered them in her heart" (Lk 2:19).

Our blessed mother reminds us that God's presence can be found in small places. If we look at creation, for example, we see the "great smallness" of God. Tiny seeds produce majestic trees. Grains of sand comprise our expansive beaches. Skinny streams of sunlight make the world sparkle.

In the seven sacraments, we encounter this sacred smallness. When drops of water are splashed over us in Baptism, we are washed in God's never-ending grace. In a simple meal of wheat and wine, we are given food to sustain our souls; in oil pressed from plants, we receive God's healing.

The seven sacraments, administered according to simple rites and liturgies of the Church, give us a glimpse of God's enormity. But if we stop, look, and listen, we can find signs of God's presence everywhere in our lives.

I remember when Sarah was a little girl; I would often take long walks with her around the lake along with her younger sisters. It was never a quick stroll because Sarah stopped every few feet to watch the ants crawl in and out of the sidewalk cracks or to sift the sand through her hands. On days when the dandelions bloomed along the shoreline, Sarah would pick the yellow weeds, one by one, as if they were fragrant roses. "For you, M-m-m-mom," she would say as she handed me the musty smelling bouquet. When we arrived home, I would place the dandelions in a Mason jar above my kitchen sink, never knowing that Sarah's small gift was God's way of saying, "Nancy, I am with you."

Now, every time I pass a field of dandelions, I remember Sarah's bouquets, and I slow down to notice the beauty of ants, sand, and warm breezes. In those moments, I find myself praising the God of littleness.

The scriptures tell us that God is "gentle and humble" (Mt 11:29). Having raised Sarah, I've come to understand that many mentally challenged persons know this humble God on a personal level.

A few years ago, I was invited to speak at a retreat for young adults with disabilities. That morning, I stood at a podium in a crowded high school gymnasium. Everywhere I looked, I saw wheelchairs, braces, thick glasses, hearing aids, and picture boards.

I had prepared a simple presentation titled "Jesus Is a Rock." With the help of some muscular volunteers, I had placed a large stone on a nearby table, a visual to show how powerful a relationship with God can be.

As I looked at the boulder, I cleared my throat. Sarah had died three years earlier, but I still shouldered the quiet and indescribable sadness of her loss. Though I had reengaged with life, each morning felt like waking up to storm clouds and never knowing when, how, or even where bolts of grief would strike. I felt distant from God and hesitant to preach about his faithfulness.

"Forget your talk," an inner voice suggested. With the exception of the humming sound from someone's oxygen tank, the room grew quiet and still.

I leaned into the microphone. "Has anyone seen God?"

My words hung in the air. I wasn't sure if anyone in the room would answer. The clock that hung on the gymnasium wall could be heard ticking.

After a few moments, a young man with cerebral palsy raised one of his stiffened arms. He was sitting in the front row, just steps away from me. "I . . . see . . . God . . . at-at . . . church," he stuttered. Everyone turned to listen to his slow, measured words.

Near the center aisle, a young man wearing a baseball cap jumped up from his chair. Dressed in a Minnesota Twins T-shirt, he bowed demonstratively, as if honoring my presence. His face bore all the telltale signs of Down syndrome, yet his slanted eyes sparkled. With a broad smile, he looked upward, scanning the high ceiling. "God is in the stars . . . B-e-e-e-e-e-you-tee-ful!" he exclaimed. With that, he shared a jubilant twirl.

Next, a young woman with thick glasses waved to me from the back, her eyes as bright as the sequins on her shirt. "I saw God yesterday at the grocery store," she said.

"Me too," someone replied.

From all corners of the room, a choir of voices echoed: "Me too! Me too!" It seemed as though everyone had recently bumped into God.

At one point, one young man simply walked to the podium and patted me on the back. His smile reminded me of a half moon, a toothy grin that lit up the rest of his face. Leaning into the microphone, he said, "You're doing a great job." With that, everyone broke into applause

"God is here," I replied, grinning.

It was then that I noticed a young woman sitting off to the side. Confined to a wheelchair, she could barely lift her head. A reverent silence filled the gym as she quietly said, "I see God everywhere."

In her, I saw a little bit of myself. I felt broken, crippled in ways that no one could see. Anyone who has grieved the loss of a loved one knows what I mean. When you lose a piece of your heart, it's hard to hold your head high when all you can feel is the hidden weight of loss.

But as I looked at this brave and beautiful young woman, and listened to her soft proclamation of faith, I felt the presence of the Lord in a way I never had before. Though I couldn't make eye contact with her, I sensed she saw much more than the gymnasium floor. With the eyes of her heart, she saw Christ and believed he was with her. And she, with all her disabilities, was inviting me to do the same.

I walked over to her and placed my hand on her shoulder. "I see God in you," I said.

For the rest of the day, I hung out with the retreatants, talking, eating snacks, and playing games in the cafeteria. It had been so long since I had felt this kind of joy, and I relished it. That day, my role at the retreat was not to deliver a talk on faith. All I needed to do was receive the sacrament of hope. My special friends had delivered Christ to me, the Christ of meekness and "pirfect" love. In them, I had found my rock-solid God.

In the scriptures, God tells us that "when you search for me, you will find me; if you seek me with all your heart" (Jer 29:13). As believers, one of our most important assignments is to uncover the presence of Christ in our lives. This call should not overwhelm us because God is always within reach. In the seven sacraments we find him in the simplest of provisions: water, bread, and wine. In the quiet whispers of a confession or in the vows we profess at the altar, the Lord draws near with outstretched arms. In holy anointings and healings, we are transfigured by the one who calls himself light.

But the Lord is always rustling through our lives like wind. He is in the seven sacraments, but God cannot restrict himself to sacred rites and rituals. Transient, he moves above us, in us, and through us as he beckons us to pay attention.

Each day, God waits for us in little places. In the manger of our home and family. In the spouses and friends who watch over us and in the babies we cradle in our arms. God comes to us meekly in the shepherds of our Church: in every humble priest, nun, and layperson who guides us on our journey of faith. In the hands we hold and kisses we share, in silent acts of kindness or unspoken prayers, and in forgiveness and mercy, the Lord of light shines like the Christmas star. In all these things, we are sanctified.

If we race through our days, we might miss the humble glory. If we move too fast, the wind of the spirit will woosh right past us. We might not see the dandelions, hear the softness of God's voice, or receive the love he pours out upon us. But if we slow down, we can stop to treasure the sacredness. And like Mary, we will ponder it in our hearts.

Acknowledgments

I wish to thank my family—Don, Christina, Rachael, and Bennett—for letting me share our story. You remain sacrament to me, sign and symbol of God's grace in my life. My thanks go out to my mother as well. You were brave to let me write about Dad's struggle with alcoholism, and I'm certain that his story will help others. And Dad, thanks for teaching me how to tell a good story. I'm sure you are cheering from heaven as this book is published by Ave Maria Press on the holy grounds of your alma mater, Notre Dame. Go Irish! To Amber Elder and Bob Hamma, thank you for your professionalism and for exemplifying literary excellence. It's been an honor to write for Ave Maria Press and to work alongside such talented people.

I'm grateful also to the good nuns who taught English at St. Catherine's University when I was in college such a long time ago, especially Sr. Bernie who gave me writing lessons in a sunlit convent. Because of you, I started believing that I might write a book someday. My appreciation goes out to the good priests who guided our family through times of joy and sorrow and grieved with us in the time that followed Sarah's passing.

In addition, I wish to thank Marybeth Lorbiecki, my longtime friend and editorial colleague. Since we met years ago in college, you have blessed my life with friendship and support. You, more than anyone, shared in the creation of this book, fine-tuning every chapter and inviting me to seize the redemption in each story. Even when I bristled at your suggestions, your remained my true friend.

And Sarah. I love you always.

Reflection Questions

These questions can be explored on your own or, if you are reading this book with others, in a group discussion.

1. Baptism

On a small table, display a clear bowl of water, a white garment, a baptismal candle, and oil for you to view.

1. At this time in your life, which of these symbols of Baptism speak to you? Why?

2. What lessons have you learned from water in your lifetime?

3. Mark Twain once said, "The two most important days in your life are the day you are born and the day you find out why." Through the sacrament of Baptism, we are saved, anointed, and set apart for God's holy purposes. What mission have you been

saved for? Are you being called to pursue that mission more intentionally?

4. Think about the challenges you have faced in your life. When have you died with Christ? In what ways have you risen to new life?

5. In the Baptismal rite, parents are reminded that it is their duty to raise their children to "keep God's commandments as Christ taught us, by loving God and our neighbor." How can we, as a Church, help support families in this duty?

6. What is the meaning of your baptismal name? How does your name affirm your identity in Christ?

Closing Reflection: If possible, play some quiet instrumental music as you read this passage from the Psalms: "The Lord is my shepherd, I shall not want. He makes me lie down in green pastures; he leads me beside still waters" (Ps 23:1–2).

After a few moments of silence, imagine yourself sitting beside a quiet stream. Invite yourself to wade through the "still waters" of God's presence as you consider these questions: Is there anything in your life that needs to be washed away? As you stand in the water, look ahead. What do you see? Where are you being led?

Close with prayer.

2. Reconciliation

Display an enlarged photo of a confessional or even a kneeler to view as you ponder these questions.

1. How does an acknowledgment of sin in the confessional differ from a prayer offered in the quietness of one's heart?

2. Why, in your opinion, do many Catholics avoid the sacrament of Reconciliation? Can this be reversed?

3. Why is choosing to forgive someone important?

4. The word absolution means to free from guilt. In what ways can guilt be debilitating physically, emotionally, and spiritually? How would freedom from guilt change the trajectory of our lives?

5. People who have been reconciled to God and others can become powerful instruments of reconciliation. Consider some of the great reconcilers in our Church. What qualities do they bear?

Closing Reflection: If possible, play some soft background music and spend some time in quiet reflection. Then read this passage from the Gospel of Matthew: "Then Peter came and said to him, 'Lord, if another member of the church sins against me, how often should I forgive? As many as seven times?' Jesus said to him, 'Not seven times, but, I tell you, seventy-seven times'" (Mt 18:21–22).

Consider how Jesus is challenging you to live out these words. In what ways are you being called to forgive seventy-seven times? After spending some time in quiet reflection, close with prayer. If possible, try to create an opportunity to go to Confession after this contemplation.

3. Eucharist

Display a loaf of bread and a cup of wine on a small table. If possible, also display a broken dish, bowl, or plate that has been repaired with glue.

1. In Japanese culture, kintsugi is the art of repairing broken pottery with a mixture of lacquer and powdered gold or silver. The process beautifies the breakage rather than disguises it. How does this art form speak to the meaning of Eucharist?

2. On the night before Jesus died, he took bread and told his disciples, "Take this, all of you, and eat of it, for this is my Body." Why are these words so important to Catholics?

3. Catholics believe that the celebration of the Eucharist unifies us in faith, life, and worship. In what areas does the Church need more unity?

4. Some have said that the Eucharist is the altar call of Catholics. Does this feel true for you? How?

5. What can persons with disabilities teach us about the Eucharist?

6. In what ways does the sacrament of the Eucharist invite us into the mystery of faith?

Closing Reflection: Read Psalm 34:18: "The Lord is near to the brokenhearted, and saves the crushed in spirit." Where have you encountered the broken Christ in your life? How does your story of suffering draw you closer to the Eucharist? Spend a few moments in quiet reflection before closing with prayer.

4. Confirmation

Display a picture of Michelangelo's painting *The Creation of Adam*.

1. Look closely at the small space that separates Adam from God. How does this space speak to you about the sacrament of Confirmation?

2. Confirmed Catholics are obligated to defend their faith by word and deed. Give some examples of Christians who have defended their faith. Have you ever been called to defend your faith? How?

3. How would you define the fear of the Lord? Is there a difference between fearing God and standing before him in awe? Explain.

4. Why is the color red such an important visual in the Liturgy of Confirmation?

5. Bishop Oscar Romero was the Archbishop of San Sal-
    vador in 1980. He spoke against poverty and torture
    of the people and was assassinated while offering
    Mass. What would you be willing to die for?

6. Is it possible for soldiers of Christ to become battle
    worn? How? What are some ways to avoid spiritual
    fatigue and exhaustion?

7. Have you ever felt the power and presence of the
    Holy Spirit? How?

Closing Reflection: Light a candle, and take a moment to
quiet yourself. If convenient, turn on a very small fan to
listen to the sound of blowing air. Invite the Holy Spirit
to be present while reading the following passage: "The
wind blows where it chooses, and you hear the sound of
it, but you do not know where it comes from or where
it goes. So it is with everyone who is born of the Spirit"
(Jn 3:8).

Think about the areas of your life that need transformation. How is the Holy Spirit calling you to be
reborn?

Close with prayer.

5. Marriage

Display a wedding gown on a table along with two
rings.

1. The word *covenant* means a formal agreement or promise. How is the sacrament of Marriage a sign of God's covenant to his people?

2. In the marriage liturgy, couples repeat these traditional vows: "I promise to be true to you in good times and bad, in sickness and in health. I will love and honor you all the days of my life." How do these vows provide couples with a firm foundation in times of hardship?

3. How can forgiveness transform a marriage relationship? A divorced relationship? A family? Share examples.

4. What unique challenges do divorced Catholics face? How can we, as the Church, be Christ to the broken families in our midst?

5. St. Teresa of Calcutta once said, "What can you do to promote peace? Go home and love your family." What do these words mean to you?

6. How does the sacrament of Marriage draw us into a deeper, more meaningful relationship with God?

Closing Reflection: Light a candle. Pass out some note cards and a few pencils. Spend some time in quiet reflection while reading the following passage: "Whoever does not love does not know God, for God is love" (1 Jn 4:8).

Think about the gift of marriage and family. In what ways are you being called to share the love of

Christ in your family? Compose a short prayer that summarizes your thoughts. If you are part of a group, collect the prayers in a basket and place before the candle.

Close with a prayer of thanksgiving for marriage and family. Ask the Lord to graciously receive your prayers and guide all families into a deeper walk of faith.

6. Holy Orders

Display a chasuble and stole on a small table.

1. Has a priest or nun touched your spiritual life? How?

2. An ordained priest is called to be a "mediator between God and the people." Look up the word "mediator" and consider its meaning in the context of priesthood.

3. Through Baptism, all believers share in the mission of Christ to be priest, prophet, and king. Give examples of how laypersons can participate in this mission.

4. Given the realities of clergy abuse, what are some ways that we can support the good priests who serve us?

5. St. Maximilian Kolbe was a Polish priest who volunteered to die in place of a stranger at a death camp

in Auschwitz during World War II. How does his sacrifice illuminate the role of ordained priests?

6. How is ordained priesthood different from everyday priesthood?

7. Reflect upon the meaning of *in persona Christi*. Think of an example of when someone has been Christ to you.

Closing Reflection: Invite participants to quiet themselves. If possible, play soft background music and light a candle. Read the following passage: "Then Mary said, 'Here am I, the servant of the Lord; let it be with me according to your word.' Then the angel departed from her" (Lk 1:38).

Pray: "Lord, we pray that you will pour out your blessings on all our priests. And we pray for those of us who serve in the everyday priesthood of Christ. May we be like Mary, willing to say yes to your plan."

If praying with a group, close with an invitation to share special intentions.

7. Anointing of the Sick

Display a bottle of chrism oil and a stole on a small table.

1. The sacrament of the Anointing of the Sick was once called Extreme Unction, meaning final anointing. In your opinion, does the idea of final anointing keep Catholics away from the sacrament? Why or why not?

2. Why is it beneficial to receive the sacrament before an illness progresses to an extreme state?

3. Give some examples from the scriptures where Jesus touched his people. Why is the laying on of hands so significant in this sacrament?

4. The sacrament of the Anointing of the Sick is not only for the physically sick but also for those who are enduring sicknesses of the heart or soul. Consider whether receiving this sacrament could help you when you are in distress.

5. Does an anointing secure one's salvation?

6. How does an anointing connect us to our community of faith?

Closing Reflection: Read the following passage from the scriptures: "For I am convinced that neither death, nor life, nor angels, nor rulers, nor things present, nor things to come, nor powers, nor height, nor depth, nor anything else in all creation, will be able to separate us from the love of God in Christ Jesus our Lord" (Rom 8:38–39).

After contemplating the passage from Romans, pray the following prayer: "Lord, we ask that the anointing we received in Baptism will continue to lead us into a deeper walk with you. Continue to anoint us with your power and strength, and guide us into your presence always. We pray for those who are sick in body, mind and soul and ask that they may never be separated from your comfort and love. Let us continue to live as your beloved children. Amen."

Nancy Jo Sullivan is a Catholic author, speaker, and retreat leader who has spent more than twenty-five years as a faith formation director and coordinator at a number of parishes in Minnesota.

Sullivan has a bachelor's degree in English with supporting courses in theology from the College of St. Catherine. She is the author of seven books, including *A Book of Grace Filled Days, What I've Learned from My Daughter,* and *Moments of Grace.* She previously worked as a contributing writer, researcher, and concept developer for Guideposts Books, as well as a contributing writer and editor for Multnomah-Random House Publishers.

The mother of three grown daughters, Sullivan lives in Richfield, Minnesota. Her eldest daughter, Sarah, is deceased, and Sullivan now finds purpose in encouraging the bereaved and supporting families who raise children with special needs.

AVE

AVE MARIA PRESS

Founded in 1865, Ave Maria Press,
a ministry of the Congregation of
Holy Cross, is a Catholic publishing
company that serves the spiritual and
formative needs of the Church and its
schools, institutions, and ministers;
Christian individuals and families; and
others seeking spiritual nourishment.

For a complete listing of titles from

Ave Maria Press

Sorin Books

Forest of Peace

Christian Classics

visit www.avemariapress.com

AVE MARIA PRESS
Notre Dame, IN
A Ministry of the United States Province of Holy Cross